Credible

The Six Leadership Conversations

Practical tools to build your influence

Possibil.com

Also by the author

A Complicated Love—Road Trip Conversations between a Straight Father and a Gay Son

If you learn about new leadership conversations
but never try them out, you will forget them.

But if you use the leadership conversations,
you will build your influence and get far better results.
And you won't forget them.

Thank you, Tracey Wimperly, for all your comments,
edits and suggestions.
I so appreciate your support and friendship over all these years.

© 2020 Dene Rossouw and Tracey Wimperly

All rights reserved. No part of this publication may be reproduced, transmitted or stored in any form or by any means without the prior written permission of the author.

The material in this publication is provided for information purposes only. This book is sold with the understanding that no one involved in this publication is attempting herein to render professional advice.

Published by Possibil.com Inc.
Sayward, Canada

Book design by Dene Rossouw
Editor: Tracey Wimperly

CredibleConversations.com
TheSixLeadershipConversations.com

CredibleConversations.com | Published by Possibil.com Consulting Inc.

Henk, Jared, Chad and Brennan, this one's for you.

Contents

The Six Leadership Conversations

Introduction to *The Six Leadership Conversations*

1. The Listening Conversation
2. The Learning Conversation
3. The Feedback Conversation
4. The Necessary Conversation
5. The Tough Conversation
6. The Mentoring Conversation

Conclusion

Dene Rossouw

The Six Leadership Conversations

Credible—The Six Leadership Conversations is a resource, guide and toolkit featuring six essential conversations to help you strengthen your influence and make a difference when you communicate. The book is built upon a foundation of skills and human interactions that have been tested and proven in a variety of environments with my clients, associates and friends over the years.

Maxim Sytch, an Associate Professor at the Stephen Ross School of Business, University of Michigan says, Informal power—which is unrelated to your formal title—can enable you to mobilize resources, drive change, and create value for the organization as well as yourself.

The way you influence others and the results you get are indicators of your skills and can make a big difference to your career and workplace environment. Your informal power of influence and your conversational competence contribute to your credibility.

Credible is a useful resource for you if you need to influence others to get things done. The tools and resources can be applied to a variety of contexts such as formal leadership in an organization, para-military leadership in police and emergency response organizations, volunteering and non-profits and even parent-child communication.

Credible is not an exhaustive treatise on leadership communication. Each chapter, or leadership conversation, is short. You can read one leadership conversation at a time, or the whole book in one sitting. As this is intended to be a highly practical resource, there are several entry points for you, depending on your needs at the time.

Although short theory bursts are sprinkled throughout, *Credible* is intended to be intensely practical to help you strengthen your authentic voice. You'll get useful tools to build your influence and conversational competence.

The Six Leadership Conversations are:

1. The Listening Conversation—helps you have a meaningful conversation with anyone who feels strongly about an issue, or wants to change or initiate something

2. The Learning Conversation—helps you coach anyone who seeks a solution to a challenge, problem or issue, by helping them take ownership of it, come to insight and take action

3. The Feedback Conversation—helps you ask for feedback from a colleague, or provide feedback to a colleague, using an approach that's specific, positive and growth-oriented

4. The Necessary Conversation—helps you have a meaningful dialogue with someone to address a challenge, resolve an issue or problem or a misunderstanding and agree on an action

5. The Tough Conversation—helps you have a structured conversation and document a course of action to resolve misunderstandings, deal with conflict and entrenched behaviours that cause disruption and deplete morale at work

6. The Mentoring Conversation—helps you mentor for results and performance using an approach that combines elements of mentoring and coaching into conversations that invite growth and possibility

I hope that after reading *Credible*, you will have internalized the intuitive steps for each of *The Six Leadership Conversations* and feel more confident expressing yourself and influencing others.

Credibility

The way you communicate is an important differentiator in how you are perceived by others. Are you *walking the talk*—engaging and interacting with people in an authentic way? Or is there a disconnect between what you say and do?

I reflect on my own conversations and none are so telling as those I've had with members of my family. One conversation in particular stands out. It took place on a five-day road trip with Jared, one of my three sons.

By way of some background, he'd surprised me by coming out. I had no idea my son was gay and we'd decided to spend some time together to talk about it.

Our conversations are recorded in my book: *A Complicated Love – Road Trip Conversations Between a Straight Father and a Gay Son*. For the better part of a week, we drove around Nova Scotia and Cape Breton and communicated. Or so I thought. On reflection, my idea of communication was steering the conversation to fit with the agenda I had in mind. Did I park judgment? No. Did I approach each conversation with an open mind? No.

On day two of our road trip I realised my approach was going nowhere. We were exploring the back roads of Cape Breton and had travelled in silence for a few hours. It wasn't the comfortable silence of a father and son just being together. It was an uncomfortable impasse.

We had covered a lot of ground—our shared history and the essence of what it means to be gay—but we were both becoming defensive. Real communication had dried up. We were both digging in our heels. I realised that having an agenda and listening just to reply was shutting down our conversation—and worse, our relationship—and any potential authentic engagement.

When Jared reminded me that I liked to portray myself as a great communicator but added, *you're not really listening to me*, I decided to toss out any pre-conceived ideas I had about homosexuality, to park judgment and to just listen to understand.

From that moment on, a shift occurred. The tension between us lifted and the conversation flowed more easily. We began to communicate more openly and deeply. As the weeks wore on, the level of trust between us grew. Neither of us dominated the conversation. We began to balance sharing our truth with a healthy respect for each other.

I've used this experience and many others as a learning facilitator and certified coach to create the framework and content for the six leadership conversations in this book.

Credible is about building your influence using six conversational tools that every leader should know how and when to use. There are no scripts. Each conversation is built around anchor points that enable listening, learning, feedback, necessary, tough and mentoring conversations.

A good sniff test is to try out each conversation away from a work environment—with a friend, partner, siblings or children. It's one thing to adopt new skills and use them on the job, but quite another to use the same skills at home. That's the ultimate testing ground. If you can seamlessly integrate the tools into a non-work environment, you will set yourself up for success at work.

If you learn about new leadership conversations in this book, but never try them out at work and home, you will forget them.
But if you use the leadership conversations in this book, you will build your influence and get far better results. And you won't forget them.

⇔ ⇔ ⇔

Closing the communication gap

There is a significant difference between what you want to tell colleagues and employees and what they want to hear. Too often, we think we've communicated, when in fact, we have simply sent out or shared information. Without allowing for an opportunity to discuss, and for the potential to establish understanding, communication has not truly occurred.

George Bernard Shaw said that *the single biggest problem in communication is the illusion that it has taken place.*

From an employee perspective, what goes on at work is often like watching a street parade. Senior management usually have a view from the curb. Middle managers have a slightly obscured vantage point and often rely on their senior managers to interpret what's going on for them. Most employees, however, have a view of the back of someone's head, offering mere peeks of the parade. Their customary viewpoint is vastly different from what leaders see.

An employee's understanding of where the company parade is headed is usually only a fragment of the full picture—influenced by their specific roles, their limited access to communication and their lack of personal power. Given their limited perspective of the company's direction, it's unrealistic to expect that employees would jump aboard any float heading who-knows-where.

Recognizing that not everyone has the advantage of a front row seat and that employees are the engine driving company success, leaders need to communicate and paint the vision in a clear and compelling way.

They must help employees see the fuller picture while influencing them to be part of the company's future direction. There's no magic to this but it requires intentional effort.

Credible will help you recognize and close communication gaps, using practical tools to have the six essential conversations of leadership.

⇔ ⇔ ⇔

Normal discussions and necessary conversations

Before jumping into *The Six Leadership Conversations*, I want to make a distinction between the conversations we have every day—normal, transactional conversations—and necessary, transformative conversations.

Normal, transactional discussions

These discussions are the transactional conversations we have every day. They can either be:

- ✧ routine information-sharing, job assignments for the day, updates, reminders, schedules, task-oriented discussions and small talk about the weather, or
- ✧ conversations that are less routine and happen in the moment, such as those involving a process such as safety, evacuation, crowd-control or steps to follow in an emergency.

Think back to the many normal discussions you have had over the past 30 days. These conversations don't usually cost you emotional energy but they are essential for the function of your group or organization. Normal, transactional discussions are effective when they are purposeful and focused.

Research has shown that when someone has experienced a traumatic event, crisis or loss and is feeling vulnerable, normal, transactional discussions or small talk is often a preferred way of building relationships because conversations centre around things people have in common. It feels familiar and safe.

With small talk, there's no expectation to go deep or disclose personal information. Little emotional energy is required to maintain these conversations. For example, a nurse can strike up a conversation with a patient (about to have a painful injection) about a common interest such as growing vegetables or orchids at home. This helps to build trust. And over time, small talk can lead to deeper, more transformational or necessary conversations.

Necessary, transformative conversations

William Isaacs, author of *Dialogue and The Art of Thinking Together*, urges us to think of dialogue as a conversation with a centre, not sides. He says dialogue *addresses problems farther 'upstream' than conventional approaches. It attempts to bring about change at the source of our thoughts and feelings.*

A necessary conversation is dialogue that requires us to suspend judgment as a pre-requisite to having a meaningful conversation. When this happens, everyone benefits because we openly share *undiscussed* parts of our thinking and feelings in a safe and supportive environment. These conversations are generative, because they make space for everyone's thoughts and feelings and build a flow of new meaning and potential, innovative actions.

What insightful, meaningful and or necessary conversations have you had recently? If you can't think of any, here's a simple test: ask yourself what conversations have you avoided? Those are often the transformational, necessary conversations that you need to have.

Sometimes necessary conversations get delayed or put off indefinitely because we don't know how to go about it. These conversations usually trigger a level of discomfort because they can involve conflict, discipline and identifying and correcting bad behaviour. They require time for preparation, and a structured approach and focus.

Credible provides the tools and approach so these conversations don't have to be avoided.

Attributes of an effective communicator

Think of people you admire who are role models when it comes to effective communication. What skills do they employ? What attributes pop first to mind? We—have

Over the years, I have found that highly effective communicators demonstrate the abilities to:
- listen to understand;
- acknowledge others with empathic responses;
- empower others;
- invite and give feedback;
- create an environment for learning and discovery;
- make people feel safe;
- engage in learning conversations;
- talk about performance and coach for results;
- help others clarify ideas and promote innovation;
- have proactive, necessary conversations;
- influence without authority;
- manage conflict successfully; and
- lead tough, persuasive and sometimes disciplinary conversations.

These attributes are essential for you as a leader. Learning about and practicing the six conversations that are described in this book will go a long way to help you bulk up your communication muscles.
I invite you to jump in and try them out.

The Six Leadership Conversations

Dene Rossouw

The Listening Conversation

The Listening Conversation
List of topics in this chapter

- When to use *The Listening Conversation*
- Listening Conversation Example 1—Stella and Kam
- Conscious listening
- Committed listening
- Generous listening
- Getting to why without asking why
- Empathy or Sympathy?
- Listening Conversation Example 2—Craig and Colleen
- Using EARS to anchor a listening conversation

The *Listening Conversation* is one of the most needed conversations and yet it's seldom done well. Too often, we don't listen, and instead, are too eager to offer an opinion or solve a problem. A listening conversation is an essential tool in your leadership toolkit. It requires that we understand its essential elements.

The Listening Conversation is the first leadership conversation. It is a dialogue of discovery and empathy built around four conversational anchors using the mnemonic EARS:

- ✧ Explore
- ✧ Acknowledge
- ✧ Reflect
- ✧ Summarize and Empathize

When to use *The Listening Conversation*

The Listening Conversation helps you have a meaningful conversation with anyone who feels strongly about an issue, or wants to change or initiate something.

Listening Conversation Example 1—Stella and Kam

Kam has worked as a bank clerk for several years. Although he's been offered opportunities to work in other areas of the company, he prefers to stay in his frontline role. He enjoys the interactions with the bank's customers and knows most by name. Time and again, customers tell his manager how much they appreciate his knowledge and warm, welcoming manner.

Because he's so tuned in to the comings and goings in the bank, Kam has observed that there are some older customers who are sometimes confused about the transactions they're making. Many wait to do their banking specifically with him, because he's known for being patient. But he's noticed a growing trend with the seniors that concerns him and he wants to run an idea past his manager, Stella.

So, Kam, I must admit I'm very curious what you wanted to talk to me about. You mentioned an idea concerning some of our senior customers?

"That's right, Stella. As you know, a lot of them aren't comfortable using online banking so they come in for help with their transactions. I think many enjoy the social interaction as well."

For sure. Many are retirees with a little more time on their hands. They aren't as rushed as so many of our other clients seem to be.

"I've noticed patterns amongst a few of our older clients and I'm convinced we have a responsibility to address it."

Tell me what you've noticed.

"Some of them are confused. I mean more than just confused about banking. They're struggling to express themselves—to find the right words—I've even noticed one or two who seem quite agitated. One of our customers I've known for five years, Mrs. Abraham, she's not the same person who used to come in and have a good old chat with me while I helped her with her transactions. She still waits to see me, but over the past few months, she seems spaced out and muddled. She was in yesterday and couldn't remember my name, or that she'd just been in and taken out some cash the day before."

Hmm, I can see why you're concerned. Does Mrs. Abraham come in with anyone or is she alone?

"Sometimes she arrives with a care aide, but the aide usually gives her space while she does her banking and then accompanies her out. I don't know very much about memory loss or dementia, but I wonder if that's what's going on?"

It does sound like something might be going on with her memory. You had some thoughts about what we could do to help her?

"I am concerned about Mrs. Abraham, but I've also observed other older customers struggling as well. There are some definite signs we should be aware of. What if someone with dementia came in and wanted to take out a huge sum of money in bills and then couldn't remember doing that? Or they misplaced the cash. There are lots of scenarios—security, trust and so on—that are alarming. So, I have an idea to address this."

I'm all ears.

"I think we should consider offering training to all our front-line staff to help them recognize and respond appropriately when dealing with a client who seems to be confused or agitated. I'm thinking of something along the lines of awareness training for tellers that would help them identify possible signs of dementia and give them some tools to help them navigate the relationship with that person."

It's obvious you've given this a lot of thought, Kam. Let me check in with you to see if I've got what you're saying: you mentioned that not only Mrs. Abraham but some of our other older customers could be showing signs of memory loss or dementia. You're concerned that some transactions could be misunderstood, forgotten or could raise alarms with the public and media about trust, fraud or financial security.

And you're suggesting we develop a customized awareness training program for frontline staff that will include tools to help them navigate the relationship with this group of customers?

"You got it, Stella."
Do you have more to add to the training idea?

"I envision the training program being facilitated internally by our people who work with seniors on a regular basis but developed in conjunction with outside experts on the subject."

I think you may be on to something, Kam. You're envisioning a training session that would be made available to all front-line staff to give them the awareness and resources to act responsibly around a customer showing signs of memory loss or dementia. And you're suggesting the workshop would be developed with the help of experts but run internally by our people who work with seniors. Have I got that right?

"Exactly! I don't know what it would cost, but maybe we could explore the idea?"

I'm going to talk to a few of my colleagues—other branch managers who might be facing the same challenges—and get their input. I'll talk to the training department at Head Office, too. Can we meet again to discuss in two weeks? Does Friday the 19th at 3 pm work for you?

"Yes, that's terrific, Stella. Thanks so much for hearing me out."

⇔ ⇔ ⇔

Conscious listening

Julian Treasure, a sound and communication expert and the author of *How to be Heard*, observes that we spend 60% of our time listening yet retain less than 25% of what we hear. And that's a serious problem. Lack of listening creates all kinds of misunderstandings and can lead to conflicts at work and home.

Treasure says that being a *conscious listener* is essential for creating understanding, building trust, managing people and for having the necessary conversations of leadership.

The idea of *conscious listening* implies that you are present in the listening moment, genuinely curious and aware of any prejudices you might have. New Zealanders have a saying, *Listen with a clear ear*. On one level this means to listen for the meaning of the message that can be obscured by accents and local dialects. On another level, listening with a clear ear is to park all pre-judgements and any impacts of a shared history you might have with a colleague or employee so as to listen deeply to what is being said—and what is not being said or implied.

Kam's story could have had a different outcome if Stella had not taken time to hear him out—to *listen with a clear ear*.

Committed listening

In addition to being a conscious listener, listening requires commitment. Coach and author Robert Hargrove says, *Masterful coaches have a way of listening that we call committed listening. Committed listening starts with a commitment to give people the gift of your presence, a high quality of time and attention.*

When your colleagues know that you are a conscious, committed listener, they feel valued. Being a role model and setting an example creates more openness for you to provide feedback and in turn, have the necessary conversations of leadership when those opportunities arise.

Simon Sinek, a motivational speaker and author of *Start with Why*, famously introduced the concept of the *golden circle*, a representation of how effective people and organizations communicate. The *golden circle* is actually three concentric circles: the outside circle represents *what* people or organizations do, the middle circle depicts *how* they do it and the inner circle is *why they do it.*

Sinek says, *Very, very few people or organizations know why they do what they do. And by 'why' I don't mean 'to make a profit. That's a result. It's always a result. By 'why,' I mean: What's your purpose? What's your cause? What's your belief? Why does your organization exist? Why do you get out of bed in the morning?*

SpaceX is a good example of an organization that's clear about its *why*: *SpaceX designs, manufactures and launches advanced rockets and spacecraft. The company was founded in 2002 to revolutionize space technology, with the ultimate goal of enabling people to live on other planets.*

Effective communicators, according to Sinek, get in touch with their driving interests—their *whys*. They learn to communicate either from the outside in—from the *how* and *what* to their *whys in* the inner circle—or from the inside out, from their *whys* to the *what* and *how in the outer circle.*

When you are clear about your own *why and if everyone is clear about the why of their organization,* it's easier to influence others and get things done. Being clear about your *whys* boosts your confidence, especially when you need to communicate with important stakeholders.

Listening, says Hargrove, is a *commitment to unearth what people passionately care about.* To truly listen is to adopt the perspective of the other person and through listening, help people return to themselves.

Generous listening

Listening to understand without replying is an essential leadership competency. It's often counter-intuitive to how we have conversations with people because our default is usually to jump in to give advice, interject with alternatives or solve things before we listen and learn about what's really going on. Being prepared to learn is an indication of a generous approach. It involves parking the urge to give advice, interjecting with alternatives, or trying to solve things. We need to listen first to gain insight into the other person's *whys* or driving interests.

If you are a leader and your day is, as Hargrove puts it, *"a big ball of twine—a tangle of problems, dilemmas, puzzles and emotional reactions,"* it is precisely in those circumstances that you need to take time, albeit counter-intuitively, to be generous and hear people out.

Generous listening or listening with a clear ear does not need to be a time-consuming process but it's a disciplined approach. It will take you on average between four to ten minutes to engage in generous and committed listening to get to someone's *whys* or interests before you ask if it's okay to provide an alternative point of view or offer a solution.

Often people have convictions and beliefs that have never been articulated in a coherent way. Curious, generous listening helps surface these interests or whys to bring clarity to a conversation.

⇔ ⇔ ⇔

Getting to why without asking why

Getting to the *whys* or the person's real interests is essential when you are engaging with someone who feels very strongly about something, has an entrenched point of view or is feeling stuck.

If you ask a *why* question too early in a listening conversation, it could be interpreted as a judgment rather than a genuine question. It's important to build trust and get a rhythm of dialogue going before asking a *why* question.
I suggest you ask three or four insightful, open-ended discovery questions (who, what, when, where or how) and then ask a leading question requiring a yes or no answer. The *yes* or *no* answer will help clarify each part of the dialogue before exploring further.

Remember how Stella listened for the *why* in her conversation with Kam without asking *why*.

When someone is heavily invested in their point of view, it can take time to get to their real *whys*. It is my experience that they are often not aware of their *whys* until you begin exploring their perspective and beliefs in a non-judgmental way.

As you follow the process of asking open-ended questions followed by a leading (yes or no) question, you will help uncover their *whys* and discover interesting insights.

Getting to why without asking why is the process of sense-making: you help make sense and clarify issues by asking insightful questions and listening without judgment. Here are a few examples of insightful open-ended questions:

- ✧ What happens when things go wrong with . . . ?
- ✧ What are your top three realistic suggestions to . . . ?
- ✧ How does this align with . . . ?
- ✧ How does this compare to . . . ?
- ✧ Who else is involved or impacted by . . . ?
- ✧ When do you feel like . . . ?
- ✧ Where are the main pressure points that . . . ?

It's important that genuine curiosity and sense-making always precede any attempt to offer solutions or make suggestions. We'll explore this in more detail when we get to the essential elements of the Learning Conversation (next chapter).

Empathy or Sympathy?

The proper use of empathy is fundamental to a listening conversation. Before exploring the *Listening Conversation* in more depth, it's important to understand the difference between empathy and sympathy.

As It Happens is a daily Canadian radio interview program that airs on CBC Radio in Canada and on various public radio stations in the United States.

The radio host interviews interesting people from all over the world each evening. Some of those interviewed are experiencing tremendous loss and live in dire, life-threatening situations.

In a typical *As It Happens* interview, the host could interview a Syrian refugee, for example, living in a camp with her two daughters and son, all under the age of six. Just before the interview goes live, the host learns that Sara, the woman about to be interviewed, had lost her husband and oldest son a few months earlier in the bombing of Aleppo in the Syrian Civil War.

The host's first words to the Syrian refugee (and many other interviewees experiencing trauma or loss) are usually:
I'm so sorry for your loss.
Twenty minutes later, the host could interview the owner of a ranch in California who has lost everything—horses, houses, barns—in the wildfires raging across the region.

The host's first words to the ranch owner are typically:
I'm so sorry for your loss.

While this much-repeated response seems to be acceptable on the *As it Happens* radio program, it's inauthentic. The host can't be genuinely sorry for the losses experienced by strangers she's never met. Or conversely, to be genuinely excited if an interviewee—a stranger—has just won the lottery. There is no doubt that the host is sincere. But if there's no existing relationship between the host and interviewees, what is being communicated comes across as an automated form of sympathy to get the uncomfortable issues over with. What's needed is empathy.

Should a leader empathise or sympathise at work? Most definitions of sympathy and empathy tend to overlap. Busy leaders are not clear about the difference and tend to conflate them. The result can be a hybrid response that is neither authentic nor effective.

Let's look at the important difference between sympathy and empathy and why knowing the difference matters in a listening conversation.

Sympathy: an act of caring or feeling for others

The origin of the word sympathy means "together with feeling." Being with another person in sympathy means you respond with an act of pathos — caring or feeling for a person or group. In the earlier example, for the radio host to express authentic sympathy, a previous relationship is required: a friendship, a working relationship or a new relationship brought about by circumstances that have connected the host with the interviewee in some way over time.

> *Sympathy costs you the energy of truly caring and feeling for the other person. And to truly care and feel for the other person, you need a relationship.*

It begs the question: how can you be sorry, sad, excited, or happy for a complete stranger?

You can try and sympathise with a stranger but it can come across as inauthentic if you say, *I'm so sorry to hear about your loss* if you do not have an existing relationship with the other person.

Sympathy explained:

- Authentic sympathy is a primal human response of caring or feeling for others.
- Sympathy is not reserved only for sadness, bad news, disaster and situations of discomfort. You can sympathise, for example, with a colleague who's won an award—*I'm so excited for you.* Or a friend who's going on a well-deserved holiday—*I'm relieved you're finally getting away.*
- Depending on the relationship you have with a person or group, authentic sympathy can cost you emotional energy or it can energize you.
- In some cases, people who regularly sympathise with a colleague can end up avoiding or resenting the relationship, because of the emotional drain on their time and energy.
- Showing authentic sympathy can also imply you are involving yourself in someone's situation and feel responsible in some way for a better outcome.
- Sympathy is an appropriate response as long as you are clear about your boundaries.
  Ask yourself, *where does this person's life end and where does mine begin?*
- Authentic sympathy—an act of caring—requires a relationship and an emotional and psychological alignment with the other person or group.

When a leader's personal boundaries are porous and not well defined—or they sympathise with and get too involved in the personal lives of their colleagues and those who report to them—it can lead to emotional burnout.

Rather than trying to respond with automated platitudes, it is far more genuine for you as a leader to communicate back your understanding of their experience and let them know they've been heard and understood. There's more to it and that's *empathy*.

Empathy—an expression of understanding

Empathy is an expression of understanding, without judgement. You do not have to agree with the other person's religion or world view or behaviour to express empathy.

Empathy happens when you sense and respond to the unique experience of another person by creating a space for that person to feel heard, valued and understood. When you are fully present in this way, you communicate your understanding of the *emotions* the person is experiencing and your understanding of what it *means* to them or the impact on them.

When you empathise, you need to resist the urge to solve the other person's problems and offer solutions. You must be content, as Arthur Ciaramicoli says in his book, *The Power of Empathy*, to *live with ambiguity* and be comfortable with your *inability to find answers* or solve problems. The more you try to help, the less you are being truly empathic and the more you are shifting into sympathy.

Dacher Keltner is a professor and social psychologist at University of California. Keltner's research shows that people who are immersed in their personal and positional power do not have the ability to express empathy. They are also unaware of the value of empathy in social relationships.

Being willing to learn and understand means you listen for the perspective of the other person—their truth—and try to understand their driving interests or whys, even though you might not agree.

Empathy is not perfunctory listening to reply or offer solutions. It's about closing psychological distance—parking positional and personal power to discover, learn and acknowledge another person or group.

Empathy is committed listening without an agenda

Empathy is a human connection that requires mindfulness and emotional intelligence to better understand and respond to the experience of another person or group.

> *Empathy costs you the energy of being fully present.*

Don't try to achieve pin-point accuracy when you empathize. If you say *that must have been disappointing for you*, they might respond with *it was not only disappointing, I was discouraged and devastated*. They will correct you or build on and bring more clarity to their experience.

Empathy explained

Empathy will cost you the energy of committed listening and being present. Please consider:

- ✧ The expression of authentic empathy can happen in an instant or take time.

- Being in another person's experience means you listen to understand the unique experience of the other person without judgement.
- When you empathize, you choose not to own the outcome or solve problems.
- Responding with authentic empathy means you do not say, *I know how you feel*.
- Holding the space for another includes silence and being present without an agenda.
- Being empathic is to listen and articulate back your understanding of the *emotion* you are sensing in the other person and your understanding of what it *means* to them.

Empathy in practice

Empathy involves listening for two elements in the other person's experience: *emotion and meaning*. Listen for:

- Emotion—identify and share your understanding of the emotion or emotions you are sensing in the other person.
- Meaning—listen for and share your understanding of what it means to the other person, or the impact on the other person.

Let's go back to the CBC radio program. I hope we can agree sympathy is inappropriate because there's no relationship between the woman in Syria (or any person just about to be interviewed) and the interviewer.

Instead of saying, *I'm so sorry for your loss* (sympathy), the host should empathize.

That means the host should begin the interview by asking questions and listening. Let's roll the tape forward and presume we have heard information about the bombing of Aleppo and Sara's escape to a refugee camp.

The host could respond: *Sara, you sound heartbroken and overwhelmed with the loss of your husband and son.* (The host reflects back her understanding of the *emotion*, i.e. what Sara is feeling.)

"Yes, it is extremely difficult for me each day. I am always crying and I miss them so much."

And later in the interview, as Sara shares more details about her situation, opportunities arise for the host to empathise about the impact or what the situation *means* for Sara.

On the one hand, you want to come to Canada and on the other, you don't want your larger family to think that you are abandoning them? (The host shares her understanding of what Sara's situation *means* for Sara and her family.)

"Yes. I want to come to Canada, but I don't want to leave my family in Aleppo. It is a very difficult decision for me."

⇔ ⇔ ⇔

Being empathic does not take more time in a conversation. It comes across as authentic and sincere. In the case of the radio interview, Sara would sense the host has made the effort to listen—helping her to feel valued, heard and understood.

Understanding the difference between sympathy and empathy is integral to best leadership practices. To seamlessly express and respond with empathy is a core leadership competency. And it's essential for an effective listening conversation.

Let's look at a workplace scenario: Toni—a colleague of yours—is an independent contractor who has been on a temporary assignment with your unit for the last year. She's a busy single mother of a five year old and volunteers at a local food bank.

Next Friday, Toni's position will be made permanent. Your team is throwing a party to celebrate her move to permanent status and to recognize the successes that she has helped your unit achieve this past year.

When you see Toni at the party, should you express sympathy or empathy? Or both?

Because you have a relationship with Toni, it's appropriate to sympathize—to genuinely feel happy or excited for her. *Toni, I'm thrilled you've been made permanent.*

It is also appropriate to empathize with Toni by listening for the two elements in her experience—*emotion* and *meaning* and to reflect it back to her.
Wow, Toni, you look so relieved and happy about the good news. (That's you, her colleague, reflecting back your understanding of the *emotion* – i.e. what Toni is feeling.)

"You bet, I'm over the moon and yes, I am so relieved."

It must take a weight off you, not having to worry how you're going to make it through each month. (That's you, her colleague, sharing your understanding of the meaning – i.e. what it means for Toni—because you know what she's been through.)

"You're so right; I had the best sleep in years after I found out I'd been made permanent."

⇔ ⇔ ⇔

Using EARS in a Listening Conversation

The Listening Conversation is a primary, fundamental leadership conversation. It is a conversation of discovery built around four anchors, more easily remembered with the mnemonic, EARS:

- ✧ Explore
- ✧ Acknowledge
- ✧ Reflect back or rephrase
- ✧ Summarize (and empathize)

You're about to read a conversation using the EARS approach between Craig, the manager, and Colleen who reports to him. Both Craig and Colleen are employees of a large technology company called Solartech.

Listening Conversation Example 2—Craig and Colleen

EXPLORE—*So Colleen, I've been hearing snippets about what you are so excited about. Finally, we have a chance to get together for a coffee so you can tell me more about what you have been thinking.*

"Ok Craig, here it is – I believe we need to seriously consider a four-day work week for our organization. That's it."

A four-day work week! What got you thinking about that, Colleen?

"I've been doing lots of research and it turns out that productivity in most white-collar organizations drops off by 78% mid-week. That means that the organization is paying for services it's not getting. Employees are basically on cruise mode by the time Friday comes around."

ACKNOWLEDGE—*That's interesting—78%. What else makes you think we should look at this?*

"For one thing, long term employee well-being and work-life balance play a huge role in the ultimate success of an organization. The happier and more energized employees are, the more productive they are."

What about our customers? They are used to 24/7 service. How do you think it would work?

"Our customer service wouldn't be affected; they will get the same 24/7 service, except we rotate our service week. We still work 40 hours a week, but we spread them over 4 days. Research has shown that service improves dramatically, customer conversations become more sincere and sales go up."

REFLECT—*I can see you are passionate about this, Colleen. Do you have enough examples and information to make a pitch to Jason?*

"Yes, I do. I have stacks of examples where it is happening right now with successful companies similar to ours like SolarSun and Innovvate. Productivity goes up by a massive 85%."

What's in it for you?

"On a personal level, I'd get to spend more quality time with my kids. But I'm also in this for the long term. I love this organization and I'd like time out from our incredibly busy schedules to think of new ways of doing things, to be more innovative."

So, what you are saying is that you want more time with your kids and some breathing room to be more innovative?

"That's it. And I'd like to see a pilot in place—a test-run with our export unit and then management can decide from there."

SUMMARIZE—*I need to be mindful of our time. So, here's what I heard you say: You believe we should consider a 4-day work week because: 1. Productivity will go up instead of drop mid-week. 2. Employees will be more energized and have a greater sense of well-being. 3. Customer service will improve because employees are not operating like robots, they can be more authentic, resulting in higher sales. And 4. You get more 'me' time – time for your kids and time to think more innovatively about the business.*

Is that more or less correct?

"You got it, Craig. Thanks for listening to my rant."

EMPATHIZE—*No rant at all, Colleen. I can see you are clearly excited about this. You've done lots of research and I know this is important to you.*

Let's meet in two weeks from now. I need to speak to a few people and give it some thought.

⇔ ⇔ ⇔

Using EARS in a listening conversation

Go back and see if you can identify the two examples where Craig used empathy in the conversation.

In the first instance, Craig empathizes with Colleen by recognizing an emotion: *I can see you are passionate about this, Colleen.* And in the second instance, Craig recognizes an emotion and what it means for Colleen: *I can see you are clearly excited about this. You've done lots of research and I know this is important to you.*

When empathy is focused and properly articulated, it blends seamlessly in a conversation and builds invisible threads of understanding and potential collaboration—the essence of a leadership conversation.

It's important to park judgment when you are listening to someone who feels strongly about something. You might disagree with their approach or point of view. Or you might feel total alignment with what they are saying and support their perspective. After you have heard them out, ask permission to share your perspective, insights or approach.

In the listening conversation example, Craig used four anchors to keep the conversation on track. The anchors are not intended to be scripts, but rather guides in the form of a memory aid using the mnemonic EARS:

EXPLORE—Use open-ended questions to explore the other person's thinking. Tony Robbins once said, *Successful people ask better questions, and as a result, they get better answers.* Ask at least three to four open-ended discovery questions (what, why, who where, when and how) for every leading or closed question. Use phrases like, *Tell me more,* or *Go on.* Be mindful that the exploratory phase of a conversation is not an interrogation, it's discovery, without judgment. There are more examples of discovery questions in the second leadership conversation, *The Learning Conversation.*

ACKNOWLEDGE—As you go deeper into the conversation, acknowledge that you are truly listening with verbal cues, body language and eye contact.

REFLECT BACK—Check your understanding of the other person's points of view by reflecting back or rephrasing as you go along:
- ✧ *What I've heard you say is . . .*
- ✧ *I want to make sure I've got this right. You said . . .*
- ✧ *You mentioned X as a determining factor, but not Y and Z, is that correct?*

Continue to probe for their *why* to get clarity without judgment. You might agree with their interests or *whys* or you might not agree. Avoid interjecting your ideas or offering alternative points of view.

SUMMARIZE—You might agree, disagree or have no opinion at all about the beliefs of the other person or group. What is important, though, is to re-express and summarize your understanding of their beliefs, interests or *whys*.

Try to list three to four key *whys* (without judgment). These should be the real beliefs, reasons or interests why this person holds a certain point of view.

At any stage during the conversation, remember to EMPATHIZE. Briefly echo back your understanding of their story, by mentioning any *emotion* you are picking up (not always evident) and what it *means* for them.

For example: *You sound excited* (the emotion you picked up). Or, *It must be wonderful to suddenly have these options available to you* (expressing your understanding of what it means for the other person). Or, *That must have been so stressful* (your understanding of the emotion the other person experienced). Or, *And to give everything up not knowing if it's going to work out must have been a real dilemma* (expressing your understanding of what it meant for the other person).

The Listening Conversation using *EARS* as four anchor points is especially effective when you are dealing with someone who feels very strongly about something or has an entrenched point of view.

Once you have heard and understood their *whys*, ask permission to bring an alternate point of view.

For example: *Can I share with you where I'm coming from? Or, Now that I understand what you feel strongly about, I'd like to provide another perspective. Is that okay?* Or, *As we've been talking, a few points come to mind. Can I share them with you?*

This can be part of the same conversation if time allows, or schedule it for a later time.

Dene Rossouw

The Learning Conversation

The Learning Conversation
List of topics in this chapter

- ✧ When to use *The Learning Conversation*
- ✧ Learning Conversation Example 1—Carla and Alex
- ✧ Facilitating a process of inquiry
- ✧ Discovery process
- ✧ The Learning Conversation in three steps
- ✧ Learning Conversation Example 2—Salman and Piya
- ✧ Nurturing innovation and competence
- ✧ Levels of competence

Encouraging learning is about empowering others through discovery and curiosity. It's also about adopting a coach approach by modeling skills, techniques and behaviours so they are caught by others, rather than just taught.

The Learning Conversation is the second leadership conversation. It is a dialogue of discovery built around three conversational anchors using the mnemonic AID:

- Analyze
- Identify
- Decide

When to use *The Learning Conversation*

The Learning Conversation helps you coach anyone who seeks a solution to a challenge, problem or issue, by helping them take ownership of it, come to insight and take action.

⇔ ⇔ ⇔

Learning Conversation Example 1—Carla and Alex

Alex had just been promoted to Manager of Corporate Communications in a large insurance company. He was excited, nervous and completely green. He had the communication chops, but little management or leadership experience. Fortunately, the company offered a mentoring program that was offered to new managers to help them learn the ropes from someone with more experience.

Alex was beyond thrilled to be paired up with a senior director from an operations area. Carla was a thoughtful, insightful leader. Alex knew of her but had never met her. She'd impressed him as a stoic, introspective and razor-sharp director which all added up to a heap of reasons to be intimidated. He showed up at the door of her office for his first meeting, clutching his notepad.

Hi, come on in! Carla gestured to the table and chairs in her office and he anxiously balanced on the edge of his seat. His mentor leaned forward, smiling warmly at Alex.

He had prepared a list of questions in anticipation of this first meeting. Carla listened for a moment and then said, *Why don't you just put your notebook away for now. Let's just get to know each other.* Alex closed his notebook and looked across at her.

So, tell me about yourself, she said.

Alex started prattling on about his departmental plans. She stopped him. *Alex, when I said, 'tell me about yourself' I meant tell me about YOU. What do you like to do in your spare time? What are your passions? We are going to be learning partners for the next six months. I hope that means we're going to freely share our thoughts about career and workplace issues. We are going to swap confidences. We need to know each other to feel comfortable enough to have those meaningful conversations.*

Everything shifted at that point. Alex relaxed and opened up. Instead of discussing business, they talked about their families and shared stories about leaders they admired.

At the end of the hour, Carla said, *Next time we'll keep getting to know each other. How about we talk about what you want to get out of this relationship and I'll tell you what I want to get out of it. Sound like a good idea?*

Alex met with Carla over the next six months and no topic was off-limits. Their conversations flowed freely, and she encouraged him to speak his mind. She openly shared her failures as much as her successes. She viewed them as learning opportunities and didn't let pride or ego get in the way of talking about how she'd messed up and what she learned as a result.

Alex learned a lot about navigating the business from Carla, but as a newbie manager, what impressed him the most was her openness and transparency. He realized that a mentor's value comes from their ability to make connections and to adopt a coach approach, so others are inspired and want to learn from them.

One of the many conversations that Alex had with Carla stood out for him: "Thanks for meeting with me again, Carla. Something has just come up in the last week and I'd like your ideas on how to solve it, if that's okay with you."
It's fine with me; tell me more.

"One of the leaders on my team—a warm-hearted, outgoing, larger-than-life personality—is driving the rest of us nuts at our team meetings."

This person is driving you all nuts? How come?

"Here's the dilemma. She's outgoing and energetic. Everyone likes her but she's also very frustrating. Although well-meaning, her ideas tend to go all over the map. Because she lacks clarity, she ends up using the meeting as a sounding board. As a result, everyone takes a back seat and lets her do her thing."

What other challenges does your colleague create?

"When she focuses on her role as a project manager, she is a visionary and really good at motivating her team. That's the upside. The downside is her team often doesn't have clarity on what their objectives or milestones are—the message gets buried in the motivation."

From your perspective, what are her main growth areas?

"I'd say to learn how to close the psychological distance between her and her team. And to see things empathically from her team's perspective. In a nutshell, she needs to become an empathic listener and then, as a visionary, to focus on tangible solutions that they own."

And her greatest strengths—what comes to mind? What does she do that's great?

"Motivation and team spirit, for sure. Her team is the most energized bunch of people we have."

How would you rate the success of these meetings on a scale of 1-10?

"I'd say five out of ten, not good at all."

What I've heard you say is you have someone on your team who is a great motivator and builds team spirit. But she lacks the skill of listening and empathy. So the success rate of those meetings is only about 50%.

"Correct."

If you had to identify one thing that would help solve this—what would it be?

"I'm thinking—just like you are mentoring me, Carla—I could do something similar and offer to mentor her for a period of six months."

Okay, tell me more.

"If I can communicate clearly why I'm inviting her into a learning partnership, hopefully she'll buy into it. Then we can work on specific skills. I don't want to lose her."

What you've come up with sounds like a practical solution. It also demonstrates your commitment to her as a colleague. Is a mentoring, learning partnership something you can commit to and build into your calendar?

"Sure, I'm excited about the idea."

Tell me why you're excited about the idea.

"First of all, I'll get to build a relationship with a colleague with a view to improving our team. Second, I want the outcome to have a positive impact for both us and the team. And third, I'll end up learning so much about leadership and mentoring."

Makes sense to me; I like your sense of clarity as to why you are excited about the idea. Okay, my next question is, when will you start?

"I'll meet with her this week and suggest a learning partnership over a period of six months."

That sounds feasible. I'd like to add your new mentoring plan to our list of projects we are working on. Are you okay with that?

"For sure, Carla, it's great to have your support."

⇔ ⇔ ⇔

If you examine the conversation between Carla and Alex, I hope you noticed that Carla (mentor) never told Alex (learning partner) what to do. The conversation was about creating clarity and ownership through insightful questions. The ownership of outcomes rests with Alex, not Carla.

⇔ ⇔ ⇔

Facilitate a process of inquiry

The purpose of having a learning conversation is to facilitate a process of inquiry into problems that others raise. The objective is not to solve to the problem, but rather to ask thought-provoking questions using the three anchor points of the Learning Conversation model—*Analyze,*

Identify, Decide—to bring insight and to encourage a decision to take action.

The dialogue in the example highlighted the approach Carla followed, as she encouraged learning with a coaching mindset. She helped Alex (her learning partner) *Analyze* the challenge or problem. Then she helped him *Identify* the key issue. Finally, she helped him *Decide* what action he should take—the ownership part.

A learning conversation should integrate two approaches that encourage learning: being instructive and being curious.

Being instructive involves sharing explicit knowledge through storytelling and teaching that helps the learning partner better understand products, processes, personalities. In other words, the what, where and how of the business.

But being instructive—where the learning partner watches, listens and hopefully learns—has its limitations. It needs to be supplemented with a more interactive approach—being curious.

Being curious is the practice of committed listening and inquiry that leads to more transformational learning—the adoption of new, insightful behaviours leading to action and better results.
An essential part of your role as a leader is to nurture learning opportunities, creating "aha" moments that are key to transformational learning. Both the mentor and learning partner benefit from the dialogue, insights and tacit knowledge that are mutually shared. Being curious is a process of discovery: asking specific questions that lead to insight and action.

I'll discuss the role of being a mentor in the last chapter, *The Mentoring Conversation*.

⇔ ⇔ ⇔

Discovery process

Writing for Harvard Business Review, Tom Pohlmann and Neethi Mary Thomas introduce four types of questions. I've renamed them and added one more to make them easier to understand, more user-friendly and aligned with my experience in coaching. The five types of discovery questions are *big picture, comparative, insightful, root cause* and *action*.

In more detail:

1. *Big picture questions* help provide a map of the environment—social, political, physical, geographical, cultural, technical—to bring perspective to a problem or challenge.
2. *Comparative questions* help bring perspective by asking questions that make comparisons with other organizations, processes, decisions, costs and so on.
3. *Insightful questions* help the listener gain insight by asking open-ended discovery questions that result in more clarity.
4. *Root cause questions* help identify key issues that bring insight to the real cause of a problem and how to find solutions; and
5. *Action questions* help evoke a commitment to accept responsibility, make changes and take action.

The discovery process—asking the five types of questions—should be part of your leadership toolkit and incorporated into all six leadership conversations, especially the learning conversation.

Let's look at integrating the discovery process into the Learning Conversation.

The Learning Conversation (AID) in three steps
Step 1—Analyze - Zoom out
Ask open questions to understand the big picture. Rephrase, reframe, summarize your understanding. Help your learning partner *analyze the problem*.

Ask *big picture* and *comparative* questions such as:
- What drives you?
- What does success look like?
- How does this compare to the cost overruns of Department C?
- What happens when you are overwhelmed?
- What happens when things go wrong?
- What is the biggest difference between their customer service and ours?
- What is your biggest challenge?
- What impact does the vision and mission have on the outcome?
- How does this align with the business plan?
- How many people are affected?
- What areas are underperforming?
- How do you recognize subtle signs that could lead to the problem?
- How much is this costing the organization?
- How do our brick and mortar facility costs compare to our biggest competitor?

Step 2—Identify - Zoom in

Turn the key issue inside out and upside down with thought-provoking questions that help your learning partner identify the key issue. Ask *insightful* and *root cause* questions such as:

- What happens when you don't speak up?
- How will saying "no" make a difference?
- What is the worst thing that could happen?
- Why is this important?
- What will happen if this is not corrected?
- What do you think is the key issue?
- Where is the pain?
- How has this strategy been working for you?
- What should you let go of?
- What drives you nuts?
- How much is this costing us each day?
- What is missing?
- What keeps you up at night?
- What are your top three realistic suggestions to solve this?
- What will make this project safer and easier?
- What would you do differently if you were in charge?
- If you had one resource to support you, what would it be?

Step 3—Decide - Take action

Help your learning partner decide to take action. Ask what they will do differently. Explore what insights have come about because of this situation. Ask about the next steps and for details about the call to action. Ask *action* questions such as:

- When will you start?
- How will you kickstart this and get it moving?

- What are your top three priorities to get the green light?
- What is your plan of action?
- What will you do differently from now on?
- How can you meet the deadline?
- What is the first thing you will do by when?
- What is the most urgent and important item to deal with right now?
- Who can you rely on for support?
- Describe the action steps you will take and by when?

Learning Conversation Example 2—Salman and Piya

You're about to read a conversation between Salman, the manager, and Piya, who reports to him. Piya has been having problems with a new software system that helps managers track what equipment is being used by employees, its serviceability status and who is responsible for it.

ANALYZE—"Hi Salman, so glad I've bumped into you. Do you have a moment?"

I'm off to a meeting in 10 minutes on the other side of town, so shoot.

"I've been put in charge of this new software system that helps track every piece of equipment that is being used by all employees—from radios to remote vehicles to cameras and so on."

Ok, Piya, I'm trying to understand. It's a software program that keeps track of all physical pieces of equipment?

"That's correct."

Is there a problem with the software?

"So here's the thing. I get the program to load the equipment taken out by staff each morning at 11 am. But when I come back a few hours later, certain pieces of equipment—some of these are very expensive—are completely missing from our database. It's like a gremlin has a vendetta against only some things, while ignoring others.

Because I know you are a trouble-shooter with a background in IT, and you have a reputation for solving problems like this, I figured you could help us out. I checked with IT and they are busy with another project and can't look at this for another month."

What's the impact when those entries are missing?

"It's just frustrating for now as we have not gone live yet. But it will have big impacts later if entries for each day are not reconciled. It will affect our auditing and our asset register. Things will show up as missing or stolen."

IDENTIFY—*What ideas do you have about why this is happening?*

"It could that the system does not recognize those pieces of equipment because employees are entering the wrong code."

If you take a closer look at that, what is the easiest way to check if your assumption is correct?

"I thought that if you have a bar code and a scanner, everything will go according to plan. But sometimes the bar code is folded or indistinct and employees have to key it in manually. They may leave off a digit or the system may not recognize their manual entries if they forget to enter their authorization key. It looks like it's been entered correctly because there's no feedback that the code is accepted or not. We're dealing with a new system that still has a few bugs."

Sounds like you are on to something.

DECIDE—*What do you think you should do next to solve this, Piya?*

"My thinking is to shadow a few employees and see exactly what they are doing—how they read the bar code number and how they enter it in the system. I'll probably pick up some clues watching them."

Go for it, Piya. Let me know how you make out. How about we check in next week Monday, say at 10 am?

"Thanks for your help, Salman. Yes, next Monday at 10 am is fine. Your questions helped bring clarity to the problem. See you then. I'm hoping to have some good news to report."

A learning conversation—as with Salman and Piya—is not an interrogation but a conversation of curiosity, leading to transformational learning: mutual discovery, identification of the actual issue and ownership of the outcome by the learning partner.

Every leader needs to feel comfortable with challenging assumptions and helping employees unlearn processes and practices that worked in the past but might no longer be applicable or true.

Nurture innovation and competence

Your colleagues, employees and learning partners see the daily impact of your organization's services on your various stakeholders and customers.

If asked, they will come up with innovative ideas on how to improve service, save money, reduce waste and increase efficiencies. Because employees do not always have the know-how, channels, confidence and personal power to put their ideas forward, learning conversations are ideal for teasing out issues, challenges and ideas that have been incubating for some time.

Levels of competence

As a leader, the goal of your learning conversations is to build and encourage confidence and competence by helping your colleagues, employees and learning partners work through four stages of learning.

The concept of four stages of learning was developed by Noel Burch. He proposed that a leader's role is to help employees develop self-awareness and competencies as they migrate through four levels of learning:

1. From *unconscious incompetence* to *conscious incompetence*
2. From *conscious incompetence* to *conscious competence*
3. From *conscious competence* to *unconscious competence*
4. Operating with *unconscious competence*

The four stages of the migration:

Stage 1—Unconscious incompetence

Your colleagues and learning partners do not understand or know how to do a particular task and do not necessarily recognize the need. They may deny the usefulness of the skill.

To move forward, they must recognize the need for development in a particular area and the value of gaining new knowledge and skills before you can really help. The length of time they spend at this stage depends on their openness, mindset and desire to learn.

Stage 2—Conscious incompetence

Though your colleagues and learning partners might not understand or know how to do something or perform a certain task, they recognize the need, as well as the value of acquiring new knowledge and skills, with your help. Allow space in your learning conversations for making mistakes. Debriefing is integral to the learning process.

Stage 3—Conscious competence

At this stage, your colleagues and learning partners understand or know how to do the task. Demonstrating the skill still requires focus and concentration. Through learning conversations, you help to break it down into steps. You notice lots of conscious involvement in executing the new knowledge and skills.

Being instructive and curious, you encourage them to stick at it, to practice and to develop competence and confidence.

Stage 4—Unconscious competence

Thanks to your encouragement and help through your learning conversations, your colleagues and learning partners have developed their skills and knowledge to the point that their competence has become second nature and can be performed easily. They feel confident and empowered and can teach it to others.

When a client signs a coaching contract with me, the contract stipulates that I will not create a dependency that encourages the client continue to look to me for advice and support. I make it clear that my goal is to *work myself out of a job*, to empower my client so there's no need for our relationship to continue beyond the objectives of the coaching agreement. Counter-intuitive? Yes. But it's the ethical thing to do as a coach.

Leaders have the same responsibility—to empower those who report to them and work themselves out of being the go-to person for everything. *The Learning Conversation*, using three conversational anchors—Analyze, Identify, Decide—is an essential leadership conversation.

Dene Rossouw

The Feedback

Conversation

The Feedback Conversation
List of topics in this chapter

- ✧ When to use *The Feedback Conversation*
- ✧ How to ask for feedback
- ✧ Feedback Conversation Example 1—Hassan and Garth (asking for feedback)
- ✧ Theory burst
- ✧ What about the praise sandwich method?
- ✧ From Growth to Great
- ✧ Potential topic areas
- ✧ How to provide feedback
- ✧ Feedback Conversation Example 2—Kerri and Jeniel (providing feedback)
- ✧ Rethinking performance reviews
- ✧ Three feedback principles

The *Feedback Conversation* is the third leadership conversation. It consists of two conversations: asking for feedback and providing feedback. Both conversations follow the same growth-centred approach. The process is called *From Growth to Great*.

The *From Growth to Great* feedback model is based on the research of Carol Dweck, Professor of Psychology at Stanford University. It's centred on a growth mindset and aims at getting feedback using two main questions on each feedback topic. The two main questions are:

1. What are my growth areas?
2. What am I doing great?

When to use *The Feedback Conversation*

The Feedback Conversation helps you ask for feedback from a colleague, or provide feedback to a colleague, using an approach that's specific, positive and growth oriented.

How to ask for feedback

Hassan is a manager of 20 employees. He wants feedback from Garth, one of the supervisors who reports to him, on two areas of his leadership: his effectiveness running meetings and his communication style around the office.

Feedback Conversation Example 1—Hassan and Garth (asking for feedback)

Thanks for being available, Garth. As I mentioned in the email, I am interviewing five people—you and two other staff who report to me, a manager in Compliance who I interact with a lot and my own manager, Sally. I am asking each person the same set of questions on two topics related to my leadership: my management of meetings and my communication style. Please be as honest as you can. Whatever you tell me is not career limiting. I want to make adjustments based on actual feedback. Is that OK with you, Garth?

"I'm totally OK with it, Hassan. This is the first time that a manager has ever asked me for my feedback."

I feel that if I want to provide feedback to my team, I need to ask how I'm doing first. I'm hoping that they see I'm serious about taking evaluations to heart. I want to initiate a shift about assessments—treat it as a valuable asset instead of a threat. And it starts with me setting the example.

I want to be respectful of your time; we have about 45 minutes. I've estimated that each question should take about 20 minutes. That should leave a few minutes for us to wrap up any other thoughts at the end.
"That's fine with me."

I want to frame the feedback of each topic in two focus areas. For example, about the way I manage meetings, I will ask you first about growth areas— things I need to do more of. Then we'll shift to things you feel I'm doing great. I know it's human nature to want to start talking about things I am doing great and maybe downplay my growth areas because I'm your manager, but please stick with me. I really want to hear your observations on the growth areas first.

"Thanks for pointing that out, Hassan. I'm willing to give it a shot."

Ok, here we go, Garth. The first topic is my management of meetings. What are growth areas for me? In other words, what are things I need to do more of to improve our meetings?

"This is difficult, seeing as you're my boss, Hassan. But here goes. When we have our meetings, a few things come to mind. One is we seldom get to voice our opinions as you tend to use up most of the airtime telling us what changes are coming down the line and encouraging us to be innovative."

Tell me more, Garth. What impact does that have on the group?

"Well, that's the second thing: people tend to become disengaged and don't feel they are expected to contribute. Ideas and insights don't get shared because it's more of a one-way information download coming from you."

I never realised I was doing this, Garth. Thanks for sharing. What should I do differently?

"I would suggest that you let other members of the team chair the meetings from time to time. You could rotate the chair and draw the quieter people in. Also, most of the updates are already in the emails we get sent. It would be better to give a short 'Reader's Digest' version of what's going on and then move on."

"I like that. What else?"

"Our staff have incredible ideas and the meetings could be more about problem solving and leveraging the power of their ideas."

I had no idea this is how staff experience the way I run meetings. Wow. Anything else?

"That's about it—oh, one more thing, it will help if you recognize the preferred gender pronoun of one of our staff, Griffin. Griffin's preferred pronoun is 'they.' Not 'she'."

Now that's something I need to be so mindful of. Thanks for telling me, Garth.

"No problem."

Being mindful of the time, what if anything, am I doing great at our meetings?

"You always start on time and we never cancel. That's a good thing because our meetings are important. Another thing you're doing great is we have a clear agenda. We know what is going to be covered and everything is documented. Oh, and you never go over time, because you are so organised."

Anything I should do more of?

"Now that you mention it, you make a point of encouraging us to be innovative. You are very supportive of us and enthusiastic—keep on doing that, for sure."

Thanks, Garth. I'm taking notes. Any suggestions on how to build on this?

"I'd make a point of including more interactivity on problem solving and leveraging innovative ideas at our meetings. Use the agenda and templates you created and ask each chair—when it's their turn—to prepare a short 5-minute presentation on a new idea, something we can use or adopt as a team."
Those are great ideas—it aligns with our mission to "make ideas work."

I'd like to move on now, if that's okay with you, to my second topic, my communication style around the office. And once again, let's start with growth areas . . .

⇔ ⇔ ⇔

Theory burst

The conversation you've just read between Hassan and Garth is an example of how to ask for feedback using the *From Growth to Great* approach. I'll go into more detail on this method in the next few pages.

Research by Erich C. Dierdorff and Robert S. Rubin, both associate professors of management in the Driehaus College of Business at DePaul University, has shown that the most popular self-assessment tools used in the workplace are not sufficient to create accurate self-awareness.

They write, *The core problem is that we're notoriously poor judges of our own capabilities.* Their research shows that high self-awareness impacts positively on teams and leads to better decisions, coordination and conflict management.

What's missing is feedback. Feedback helps to build more accurate self-awareness and provides a perspective for those who tend to over-rate or under-rate their competencies and impact at work.

To emphasize the importance of increasing self-awareness and reducing blind spots, let's use the analogy of binoculars. Binoculars have two telescopes, each presenting an image to one eye. When the lenses are properly focused, your brain blends the two images into one.

Based broadly on the top left and right quadrants of the Johari Window, designed by Joseph Luft and Harrington Ingham:

- ✧ The left telescope is your open position—things that are known by you and also seen and acknowledged by others. To see clearly, it requires a habit of continuous focus, curiosity and openness.
- ✧ The right telescope represents your blind spots—things that are not known by you but seen and acknowledged by others. To create self-awareness, it requires a habit of refocusing, asking for feedback and then making adjustments based on that feedback.

When your left telescope—your open position—is blended with your right telescope—refocusing on behaviours that reduce blind spots—you have more clarity and increased self-awareness.

What about the *praise sandwich* method?

The *praise sandwich* method of feedback has been adopted by many leaders and is used frequently. You're likely familiar with the format: positive, negative, positive.

Here's an example—Joni gives feedback to Vita on her presentation to management:

First off, Vita, great work—I think your presentation was well received by the management team. I didn't hear anything negative from the VP or the CFO.

That's a relief, Joni. I wasn't sure how to read them as I went along. They seemed to be paying attention but you can never tell. They left before the question period which did worry me a bit.

I wouldn't read too much into that, Vita. They're both extremely busy and were probably rushing off to another meeting.

I did hear a few murmurs though from some of the other folk who were there.

Okay. How come they never approached me?

Not sure, but I received an email—I'm not getting into names but here's the gist of it:
"too long," "not enough research," "another crazy employee trying to impress management" and "waste of time, learned nothing."

Wow.

Now, I don't agree with all of those comments. My only feedback to you is to keep it short, push one idea and leave the rest for another time.

But Joni, to promote one idea and leave the others would do a disservice to the company as they are all intertwined.

I know, but we all have a limited attention span, even senior management. You gotta learn to go with the flow, Vita.

Overall, I think you did a good job. You spent a lot of time on it and you know, you can't please everybody. Steve Jobs didn't give up after his first presentation to decision-makers, did he? Just ignore those other comments and go for it, Vita.

⇔ ⇔ ⇔

How do you think Vita was feeling as she walked away from her feedback session with Joni?
Motivated? Encouraged? Inspired? Is she aware of specific growth areas to work on? Or is Vita demotivated, discouraged and wounded?

With the praise sandwich approach, employees are fed a tidbit of positive stuff, followed by some bad stuff. The conversation ends with a sweetener—a topping of positive syrup that usually comes across as disingenuous and manipulative.

To quote author and social scientist, Joseph Grenny, employees—like Vita—on the receiving end of a praise sandwich feedback session often feel like they have been *feedsmacked*.

⇔ ⇔ ⇔

From Growth to Great

The *From Growth to Great* feedback model is based on a growth mindset and aims at getting feedback using two main questions per topic:

1. What are my growth areas?
2. What am I doing great?

The *From Growth to Great* approach is a departure from the *praise sandwich* method. It eliminates the perception of feedback as either positive or negative. If you reflect on the feedback conversation between Hassan and Garth, you will notice that Hassan positioned the process as starting with *growth* first and then moving to *great*.

In more detail, asking for feedback using *From Growth to Great* uses two main questions and a minimum of one secondary question for each of the *From Growth* or *Great* questions.

Asking for feedback—facilitating effective meetings at work (for example)

1. What are *Growth Areas* for me?
   - What do you suggest I do more of to improve this?
2. What areas am I *Doing Great*?
   - How can I build on this?

When asking for feedback, it's important to resist the urge—usually coming from the person providing you with feedback—to shift the conversation to things you are doing great before addressing the growth areas. Each of the two secondary questions in the *asking for feedback* process is an opportunity to dig deeper to encourage growth and inspire action.

After you've moved to things you are doing great, ask more questions such as, *What do you like about it?* and *What do you suggest I continue doing?*

When asking for or providing feedback, always create a safe space for open dialogue. A safe space can be:

- A physical location that eliminates eavesdropping, for example; or
- An environment of psychological safety where both participants in the dialogue feel a sense of respect and trust so they have the freedom to be vulnerable and can speak truthfully.

When people feel safe, it boosts their confidence to be specific about growth areas that lead to change.

The *From Growth to Great* feedback process is all about growth. The questions you ask your colleagues, clients and direct reports should provide you with deep insight that will help you take corrective action (growth areas) and build on certain practices identified by your colleagues (things you're doing great). It also provides proactive professional proof and substance for your performance review.

In anticipation of having a series of asking-for-feedback conversations, make a list of at least three to five people: include people who report to you, a colleague and your own manager. Try to include someone who drives you nuts or someone with whom you don't get on too well.

Resist the urge to create a shopping list of feedback topics. Limit your session to a maximum of three topics and make every effort to have your feedback sessions in-person, or use a virtual video platform or other suitable social media platform that enables in-person dialogue.

Make appointments with each person and send them the topics you want feedback on in advance of the session. This lets them know you are serious about asking for feedback and helps them prepare. Remember to thank your colleagues for setting aside time to provide you with feedback.

Potential topic areas

Ask for feedback on the ways you:
1. Lead the team
2. Communicate at work
3. Manage challenging personalities
4. Solve problems
5. Manage change
6. Implement the business plan
7. Set the mission and vision
8. Delegate responsibilities
9. Inspire others to innovate
10. Organize your life at work

How to provide feedback

Five supervisors report to Kerri. In this example, Kerri is providing feedback to one of her supervisors, Jeniel, on his leadership style.

Feedback Conversation Example 2—Kerri and Jeniel (providing feedback)

Thanks for being here, Jeniel. As I mentioned in the email, I am providing feedback to all five supervisors who report to me. You will recall, two months ago, I asked you all for feedback on my leadership style. I found it was very insightful and hope after our session you will find it useful as well.

Just to let you know, everything we talk about is confidential. Is that okay, Jeniel?"

"No problem, Kerri."

I mentioned in the email that we have about 45 minutes. You sent me two topics you want feedback on. I understand you have already asked the people who report to you to give you feedback on those topics. I have added a third. So, the three topics are: having necessary conversations at work, your presentations skills and your general leadership style. Are you comfortable with the topics and the process, Jeniel?

"Totally comfortable Kerri, let's do it."

Let's start with necessary conversations at work. I'd like to focus on growth areas first. Then we'll move on to things you're doing great. What are growth areas for you?

"Based on feedback from my staff and my own insights, I realised—and this is partly a cultural thing—that I tend to avoid having necessary conversations with some staff because it makes me feel uncomfortable. I also thought that I was being disrespectful by talking about certain behaviours."

What have you done—and I know you have worked on this—to turn things around?

"I knew I was avoiding it, but it was only when I asked my staff for feedback that I realised I had to do something. They pointed out that everyone knew that a few staff always bent the rules like not showing up on time. And management—me in this case—looked the other way. At least that was their perception. I took that feedback to heart and had the necessary conversations with those staff to bring things back in line."

How did you feel after you made the change?

"I felt empowered and immediately noticed a change with all staff. Word spread around and everyone started pulling their weight."

That's good to hear, Jeniel. Can I share with you my perspective on this? I knew you were so busy with the change project and you had your head down just to make it through each day. The last thing you wanted was to address issues that were uncomfortable. But in avoiding them, things got worse as you ended carrying more of the load while others slacked off.

The growth area from my perspective is to make necessary conversations part of your leadership DNA. Just make the appointments, that's half the battle. I get the impression you started to do that already?

"You're right, Kerri, I have."

OK, that leads us to things you are doing great in this area. What did you learn?

"Since I got feedback from my staff, I now make a habit of listening to them—listening to understand, not reply and when appropriate, having necessary conversations. Some of these are informal and others are more formal. But I use the same structure to guide me in all these conversations. And I am seeing a difference."

What else are you doing to reinforce and build on this new practice, Jeniel?

"A simple thing really. When I know I need to have a necessary conversation with a staff member, instead of agonizing about it like before, I don't procrastinate. I make the appointment. As you said, when it's in both of our calendars, that's half of the issue solved already."

I'm impressed to hear that you've created a habit of putting your appointments in your calendar. Once they're there, you're committed. That's a good habit.

"It's one way of setting myself up for the conversation. I also add notes to the calendar entry. Then when the time comes to have the necessary conversation, I read my notes and print out the guide. It's becoming easier, the more conversations I have."

Well done, Jeniel. Can I share with you my observations on what you're doing great?

"Go ahead."

What I've noticed over the past few months is an openness amongst your team. You've set an example and now they have permission to do the same—to have necessary conversations so everyone is accountable and on the same page.

"Thanks, Kerri."

That's something you are doing really great. Please keep doing this. People are noticing.
I'd like to move on now to presentation skills . . .

⇔ ⇔ ⇔

The conversation you've just read between Kerri and Jeniel is an example of how to provide feedback using the *From Growth to Great* approach.

You will notice that Kerri positioned the process starting with growth first and then moved to things Jeniel is doing well.

Similar to *asking for feedback*, providing feedback uses the same two *From Growth to Great* questions. But there is a key difference: Kerri (the person providing the feedback) first asks Jeniel (the person receiving the feedback) what he believes his growth areas are. Then Kerri asks for Jeniel's permission to provide her insights on his growth areas.

When the conversation moves to things Jeniel is doing great, Kerri once again first asks him for his input as to what he thinks he's doing great before providing her observations on what she thinks he's doing great.

And of course, secondary, follow-up questions are essential to get to the details and help make the dialogue interactive.

In summary, providing feedback using the *From Growth to Great* method uses two main questions and secondary questions.

Providing feedback—having necessary conversations with staff at work (for example)

1. What are *Growth Areas* for you?
   a. What should you do more to improve this?
   b. Some of my insights on growth areas for you are . . .
2. What areas are you *Doing Great*?
   a. How can you build on this?
   b. You are doing great in these areas . . .
   c. Please keep doing . . .

Wrap up the feedback conversation with three actions. Ask your colleague to commit to one thing they will:

- ✧ Keep doing
- ✧ Stop doing
- ✧ Start doing

Finally, agree on a date to review progress on the feedback topic and the actions.

Rethinking performance reviews

With some exceptions, managers in today's organizations no longer use an industrial age production line scoring system to pin an employee's annual performance to a number between one and five. That's a good thing.

Employees shouldn't be constrained to archaic performance management metrics that are unrelated to what they do and the value they bring. Annual measures of performance with limited feedback is usually harmful, irrelevant and out of step with an ever-changing and dynamic environment.

Regular feedback—*From Growth to Great*—should be the norm for supporting learning, development and performance management. If your organization requires some form of performance measures or standards of compliance, regular feedback will ensure there are no surprises when the time comes to review an employee's performance against those measures or standards. If your organization still has a variation of the annual performance review, regular feedback throughout the year will make the grading system more dynamic and relevant.

Instead of using an impersonal and archaic scoring system, organizational and personal growth goals should focus on three growth-oriented criteria for assessing progress on key result areas:

- ✧ Not there yet
- ✧ Nearly there
- ✧ Nailed it!

These criteria are based on the growth mindset thinking espoused by Carol Dweck. In her TED Talk, the *Power of Yet*, she says *building a bridge to yet* places a person on a learning curve, introducing hope. The concept of "yet" gives people *a path into the future* instead of judgment on their performance.

Three feedback principles
1. Be respectful and truthful

Joseph Grenny—a New York Times bestselling author and social scientist—distinguishes between feedback (conversations that foster growth) and blowback (conversations that lead to grudges and create wounds).

Make a point of parking judgment. Don't use the session to vent frustrations, especially if you have a level of authority over the person you are meeting with. The *From Growth to Great* approach is intended to encourage growth and is not an opportunity to express grudges.

Avoid sugar-coating feedback and asking softball questions such as *How am I doing?* At the same time, never deliver feedback in a way that bruises relationships. Have the courage to ask uncomfortable behavioral questions such as *How does my communication style impact those around me?*
Be truthful and respectful of the other person when providing feedback. Ask permission to share your perspective and always ensure you create an environment that is non-threatening so your colleague feels safe.

Be aware of power imbalances—such as manager and employee dynamics—when setting up a *Feedback Conversation*. When people feel safe, it enhances learning and contributes to more permanent performance outcomes.

2. Be curious and empathic

When you are genuinely curious, you build trust and people let go of being defensive. Ask at least three to four open-ended discovery questions (what, why, who where, when and how) for every leading or closed question. Use phrases like, "Tell me more," or "Go on." Be mindful that being curious is not an interrogation: it's discovery, without judgment.

Dr. Arthur P. Ciaramicoli, clinical psychologist and author of *The Power of Empathy*, defines empathy as your ability to understand and respond to the unique experiences of another. Building on Ciaramicoli's idea, the practice of empathy involves listening for two elements in the other person's experience: emotion and meaning (as discussed in the *Listening Conversation*).

Empathy, vulnerability and authenticity can't be faked. When you are empathic and genuinely curious, your colleagues perceive your non-verbal communication to be aligned with and congruent with your words. This invites colleagues to participate and contributes enormously to meaningful feedback interactions.

3. Be organised and consistent

When you decide to implement regular feedback conversations amongst the members of your team, you'll find it's a rewarding and energizing practice. But it won't happen unless it's supported and driven by the leadership. And it needs to be organised. Someone needs to be responsible for the feedback calendar so that all feedback sessions are posted in an open calendar. This sends a message that the practice of asking for and providing applies to everyone, including leadership.

Be clear about the purpose of the feedback session and be open for new perspectives. Always share how the feedback process will unfold before asking for or providing any content. Frame the process as beginning with growth areas first and then moving to things that are great. If you are consistent about asking for feedback so you can adjust your leadership style, it rubs off on the whole team.

If you encourage your team to ask for and provide feedback to colleagues and managers regularly instead of once a year at a performance review, it will become part of the culture. Then feedback will not be perceived as a threat but welcomed because it's framed as essential for leadership growth and empowerment.

When you want feedback on something or an issue comes up that needs to be addressed, feedback should also happen in the moment, not a month or six months later. When you consistently reduce the lag time between knowing you need to provide feedback and actually doing it, people notice. This contributes to the overall psychological health and morale of your department or organization.

Dene Rossouw

The Necessary Conversation

The Necessary Conversation
List of topics in this chapter

- When to use *The Necessary Conversation*
- Necessary Conversation Example 1—Sanaaz and Bernadette
- Theory burst
- Necessary Conversation Example 2—Craig and Maxine
- The four conversation anchors: Notice, Think, Feel and Act (NTFA)
- Two rules for every necessary conversation
- Low or High Dialogue Leadership
- Microaggressions
- Rut and river stories
- Recognize personality preferences
- Necessary Conversation Example 3—Katia and Pendra
- Ten potential necessary conversations

When an issue comes up that needs to be addressed in the moment, *The Necessary Conversation* is one of the most important, yet neglected conversations we need to have. It is a fundamental and essential tool in your leadership toolbox.

The Necessary Conversation is the fourth leadership conversation. Based on the work of Gervase Bushe, it is a dialogue of resolution built around four conversational anchors using the acronym NTFA:

- Notice
- Think
- Feel
- Act

When to use *The Necessary Conversation*

All of the conversations in this book are important for leaders. *The Necessary Conversation* is the conversation that is most needed yet most often avoided. *The Necessary Conversation* helps you have a meaningful dialogue with someone to address a challenge, resolve an issue or problem or a misunderstanding and agree on an action.

Necessary Conversation Example 1—Sanaaz and Bernadette

Sanaaz works for a large financial institution in a middle management position. She reports to Bernadette, a Vice President. Every Wednesday morning, the two meet for a half hour one-on-one.

Sanaaz looks forward to these meetings and always arrives at the appointed time at Bernadette's office with a list of topics to discuss. They sit across a small table from each other where Sanaaz launches into her update.

These sessions are becoming more and more unsatisfying for Sanaaz because she can't seem to get Bernadette's full attention. Bernadette glances at her phone, gets distracted by people walking past the window, doodles on a pad of paper and more. There is little dialogue, almost no eye contact and a whole lot of frustration. Sanaaz leaves the meetings feeling disgruntled and hurt by her boss's dismissive behaviour.

After many weeks of mediocre meetings that feel like a waste of time, Sanaaz knows she has to speak up and address this with Bernadette. At their next scheduled one-on-one, Sanaaz raises the issue.

Bernadette, before I give you my update, I'm hoping we could talk about the effectiveness of these one-on-one sessions. Are you open to that?

"Sure, what's on your mind?"

Well, we've been meeting every week for a couple of months and while I appreciate the opportunity for these one-on-ones, I've noticed—and I could be totally wrong about this—that you seem pre-occupied. I feel as if I'm just reeling off a list of the projects my team is working on and don't seem to be getting your attention.

"Okay. Go on."

When I tell you about what we're working on and our progress, I get the impression I'm competing with more important things on your mind. To be honest, I'm feeling a bit demotivated.

"What makes you feel that way?"

Well, I notice that you look at your phone a lot and at people walking by your office behind me. There's not much eye contact between us. I find myself wondering if I'm boring you or if you're expecting something else from me at these meetings. What are your thoughts on this?

"You're right. Our meetings are not as productive or efficient as they could be."

So, I'm not imagining it. Can you tell me what's going on for you—what do you think?

"We only have a half hour together, Sanaaz, and what I'd like from you is a high-level overview of what you're working on. I don't need all the minutiae and commentary about who said what to whom. Less is more, Sanaaz."

I assumed you would want to understand our thinking around various strategies and how we came up with the approaches we did.

"To a point. But honestly, Sanaaz, I hired you because you're smart and you have smart people working for you. I know you were being super conscientious about giving me all the details. But I don't need all that information, I just need to know what decisions you have made, what you need from me, what it's going to cost, and the risks if we go ahead."

Ok, I'm feeling relieved that we are having this conversation. Now I have a better understanding of what you've been thinking and what you need. I know we both want to make sure we're making good use of our time.

"Yes, there's a lot going on. I have so many meetings. But I don't want you to feel as if you can't share some important background information with me. Perhaps you could indicate that you want to have that discussion beforehand. It will help us stay focused."

How about from now on, I'll put together an agenda of items I want to bring to your attention and send it to you the day before? That way, my list of talking points won't be a surprise and you'll have some advance notice of any deeper discussion items. Does that make sense?

"That sounds like a good plan. If you send me a brief agenda ahead of time, that would be appreciated."

Thanks for being receptive to this conversation, Bernadette. I'll be more aware of using our time productively.

"And thanks for bringing up the topic of our weekly meetings. I should have said something sooner. I'm glad you took the initiative and had the courage to speak up about it."

⇔ ⇔ ⇔

Theory burst

David Bohm—one of the most significant theoretical physicists of the 20th century—reminds us that there is a difference between a discussion and dialogue. A discussion is more transactional and tactical. The conversations that Sanaaz was having with Bernadette had limited value for Bernadette because her expectations—a high-level summary and actions—were not being met. Sanaaz was frustrated because she felt Bernadette was not engaged at all during their meetings.

When Sanaaz plucked up the courage to have a necessary conversation with Bernadette, she initiated a shift from their routine discussions—that were not working for either of them—to more meaningful dialogue.

Although by no means an example of deep dialogue, her conversation with Bernadette helped build a connection with her boss. As per Bohm's explanation, something different happened when Sanaaz chose to speak up and share her true experience. In effect, when Sanaaz described what she was noticing, thinking, feeling and the action she wanted out of their meetings, their relationship became more transparent and authentic.

Gervase Bushe, professor of leadership and organization development at the Beedie School of Business at Simon Fraser University, introduced *The Experience Cube* in his book, *Clear Leadership,* as a way of understanding four elements of experience: observing, thinking, feeling and wanting. I have adapted the *Experience Cube* slightly and talk about four *anchors* that help keep a conversation on track. If you scan the conversation between Sanaaz and Bernadette, you will see the four anchors embedded in the conversation. Sanaaz had a *Necessary Conversation* with Bernadette and communicated what she was Noticing, Thinking, Feeling and the Action she wanted.

The four anchors—Notice, Think, Feel and Act (NTFA)—are not scripts but "departure points" for the person leading or initiating a conversation. It's crucial that the person leading the conversation, in this case Sanaaz, brings Bernadette fully into the conversation.

When the four anchors—Notice, Think, Feel and Act—are used interchangeably by both Bernadette and Sanaaz, it becomes a more effective necessary conversation. Note that when Sanaaz shares what she is noticing, thinking, feeling and the action she wants (in any order according to the flow of the conversation), Sanaaz also needs to be curious about what Bernadette is noticing, thinking, feeling and the action she wants.

Using the four anchors as departure points, while parking judgment, help to keep a conversation on track without coming across as scripted. And at the same time builds rapport. Laurence and Emily Alison, authors of *The Four Ways to Read People*, say that rapport *is not only the bedrock of successful relationships, but also provides the best path to securing information from difficult people.*

A *Necessary Conversation* can help both participants gain clarity about the issue or problem, reach understanding and resolve the issue. But it's not a guarantee that even though an issue was resolved, that the conversation had evolved into dialogue. When dialogue and rapport happens, it evokes trust, more transparency and sharing of truth without fear of judgment.

William Issacs, author of *Dialogue and the Art of Thinking Together* and a lecturer at MIT's Sloan School of Management says, *Dialogue, practiced well, has a far more radical edge that encourages us to learn to tell the truth about our own and others' inconsistencies . . . to enable us to transform them.*

Necessary Conversation Example 2—Craig and Maxine

Before we expand on each of the anchors, let's look at another example: Craig, a supervisor in a large inner-city municipality needs to address a touchy subject with Maxine, his manager. Her calendar view is not accessible to him and his colleagues and that's created some issues for him and his colleagues.

Thanks for being available, Maxine. I set up this meeting because I wanted to speak to you about the open access calendar that all our staff use.

"OK, so what's on your mind?"

NOTICE—*Well Maxine, I've noticed that in the past, we all had access to each other's calendars and then for the past three months, your calendar seems blocked. Are you aware of that, Maxine?*

"Yes, Craig, I disabled that function because I didn't want everyone peeking in on my private affairs. You know I'm going through a divorce, but no one else does and I don't want them seeing appointments for lawyers and Family Services and so on."

THINK—*I think it was very brave of you to mention that, Maxine. I thought it was something like that. Can I share with you what I've been thinking but not saying?*

"Go ahead."

I've been thinking that because we don't have access any more, staff are starting to wonder what's going on. In the absence of an explanation, soon they're going to make up stories.

"I hope not. They should be above that and you know what? They should mind their own business."

What thoughts do you have that could lessen the chance of staff speculating about this change in access to your calendar?

"I haven't given it any thought, but now that you mention it, I don't want staff making up stories about what's going on with my life."

FEEL—*Maxine, I'm really concerned that sooner or later they will find out what's going on because people talk. Does that worry you as well? You definitely don't need any more stress in your life right now.*

"You're right Craig, what ideas do you have?"

A couple of things. It's important that staff have access to your calendar and what's important is that you don't feel exposed to the whole world.

"Right."

ACT—*So, here's a suggestion. Did you know that you can have more than one calendar in Outlook?*

"No, I didn't. Tell me more."

You can have your private calendar that no one else can see and sync it with your iPhone. And you can have the staff calendar that everyone can see and also sync it with your iPhone. Both are controlled by you.

"Sounds interesting."

So how about we set up a time and I show you how to create your private calendar, and then restore the work calendar to open access?

"Sounds like a plan, Craig. Thanks for bringing this up; I know it's important we sort it out. I just haven't had the emotional energy to go there till now."

Now that you've read the conversation, please review the four anchors that Craig used to guide the conversation to a successful outcome.

⇔ ⇔ ⇔

The four anchors: Notice, Think, Feel and Act (NTFA)

The four anchors are fundamental for necessary conversations. Each one *anchors* the conversation around a key conversational element, creating the potential for truth-telling and genuine curiosity to happen.

Notice—the first anchor

One of the easiest entry points into a necessary conversation is to begin with what you've noticed or are noticing at the time. Or, you can begin a conversation by asking what your colleague (the other person in the conversation) has noticed or is noticing at the time of the conversation.

We might think we are sharing just what we've noticed, but we are prone to bias. We make up stories.

Most people in leadership should be familiar with the *Ladder of Inference*, first put forward by organizational psychologist, Chris Argyris. The *Ladder of Inference* illustrates how we make assumptions and reinforce them by adopting beliefs that lead to actions based on wrong assumptions. Here's an example:

Let's follow Tania as she arrives at work at 8:30 am.

1. She notices stuff: *Everyone is in a meeting upstairs in the boardroom.*
2. She interprets that info: *I wonder why I was not invited?*
3. She adds her own meaning to it: *Maybe they don't want me here anymore.*
4. She assumes things about that info: *I'm sure it's about the cost overruns on the project.*
5. She draws conclusions based on that info: *I don't think they value the work I put into this project.*
6. She adopts a belief about it: *Dad always told me never to trust anyone. I should never have trusted their "support."*
7. She takes actions based on her belief: *I think I'll email my manager and let her know it's not fair that I'm being excluded after all the work I've done.*

Unbeknownst to Tania, she was emailed about the early meeting but her email was not delivered. Tania updated her iPad software the night before and was unaware it affected her work email.

If Tania sends the email to her boss, she could embarrass herself by saying: *I noticed that when I arrived, everyone was in the meeting already and I'm wondering why I was not invited.*

Although the example above is a simple illustration of the way we draw inferences and make assumptions, we act out versions of this all the time.

As you prepare to have necessary and crucial conversations, be mindful of the assumptions you make beforehand and the story you believe about the situation or the other person. Even though you might say to yourself that you have seen this 1,000 times before, or you know this person well, the story you make up can influence your approach and colour the outcome.

Being self-aware is a crucial leadership skill. Before you begin a necessary conversation, play back what you've observed or are observing and temper it with a reality check. Say to yourself, *I could be wrong, what am I missing?* Or, *what judgments or prejudice am I adding that's not relevant or true to the situation?*

An easier way to navigate this when you're having the conversation is to say something like: *I could be wrong about this, so please correct me. This is what I've noticed over the past few weeks . . . What's your perspective? How do you see it?*

Think—the second anchor

When you give yourself permission to communicate clearly what you are thinking, you establish distinct boundaries for yourself and the other person as you communicate. If your thoughts are clearly articulated, you eliminate the fog of innuendo, insinuation, and mixed messages because you're placing your thoughts in a transparent container, as it were. It helps to set a boundary around what you are thinking.

As you communicate what you are thinking, you create imaginary boundary lines around a container of thought. This helps to clarify where your thinking ends and the other person's thinking begins. It also helps to bring clarity, because the container is open for inspection at any time.

Dr. Henry Cloud, author and expert on personal boundaries says, *Boundaries define us. They define what is me and what is not me. A boundary shows me where I end and someone else begins, leading me to a sense of ownership. We must own our thoughts and clarify distorted thinking.*

Being curious about the other person's thoughts and expressing your own can initiate an interactive rhythm that leads to dialogue, as long as no one doubles down on their point of view as the *truth*.

When you bring your thoughts into the conversation, don't confuse thoughts with feelings. For example, your colleague could say: *I feel we are reaching a point of no return.* Maybe your colleague is responding to a gut instinct or a sensation. For it to be a *feeling* statement, they need to find words that describe the feeling: *I'm worried/concerned we are reaching a point of no return.* Or, *I'm feeling desperate as we inch towards a point of no return.*

We all vary in the ways we share our thoughts. Sometimes we share spontaneously—when the topic triggers ideas or a reaction—and at other times, we respond in a more measured way. Neither is wrong or right, but it's a good idea to let those with whom you have regular conversations understand your communication style.

If your style of communicating is to *talk to think*, let the other participants know that your process is to get clarity as you talk. And tell them it's ok to challenge you, to ask for clarity and provide feedback.

If your preferred style is to *think to talk*, don't wait for absolute clarity or try and think through the perfect response or idea before you speak. Tell the other participants when you need time to think something through. If the topic is complex and needs a lot of reflection, stagger your conversations into a series of necessary conversations.

If you withhold what you're thinking, or only disclose slivers of your thoughts, others will fill in the gaps or make assumptions based on the absence of information or your verbal cues and body language. They will most often get it wrong.

Your willingness to describe how you interpret your experience and thoughts to others is key to having successful necessary conversations. And the flipside—being equally curious about the thinking and experiences of the other person - is essential.

Let's go back to the conversation between Craig and his manager, Maxine:

Can I share with you what I've been thinking but not saying? (Craig)

"Go ahead." (Maxine)

I've been thinking that because we don't have access any more, staff are starting to wonder what's going on. In the absence of an explanation, soon they're going to make up stories. (Craig shares his thinking with his manager, Maxine. He draws a boundary line around his thoughts to clarify: in the absence of an explanation, staff are going to make up stories).

"I hope not. They should be above that and you know what? They should mind their own business." (At this stage Maxine is still defensive.)

What thoughts do you have that could lessen the chance of staff speculating about this change in access to your calendar? (To clarify things further, and to place a container around Maxine's thinking, Craig asks Maxine for her thoughts.)

This short snippet serves to illustrate the value of the second anchor, bringing our thoughts into every necessary conversation.

Feel—the third anchor

Until recently, leaders didn't often express how they felt about something. Admitting they felt surprised, hesitant, uneasy, optimistic, etc. was perceived as inappropriate for the workplace. Some leaders believed any expression of emotion was a sign of weakness.

We now know that if you identify and communicate what you are feeling, it's not only an indication of internal coherence, it's a sign of strength and leadership competence.

The workplace is a potent incubator for emotions. Stress and frustration usually top the list. When you don't give yourself permission to express what's really going on or how you are feeling, it finds a way of leaking out in your body language and attitude.

Gervase Bushe says *body sensations are the most primal form of experience, contain lots of important information, and have a big impact on how we think, what we want and what we do.* He goes on to say that emotions are *sensations with a message.*

Whether you are feeling disappointed or optimistic about a project, when you don't give yourself permission to say what's really going on, your colleagues will *read the news*—leaks from your facial expressions and body language—and make up their own story about what's happening.

Your emotions function as an internal radar. Learning to recognize that you are feeling something and to describe what you are feeling takes practice. Once you can label the feeling, you can express what's true for you.

Susan David, author of *Emotional Agility*, tells us *it's not always easy to do, because our emotions are not always reliable. In some situations, they help us cut through pretenses and posturing, working as a kind of internal radar to give us the most accurate and insightful read into what's really going on in a situation. But in other situations, emotions dredge up old business, confusing our perception of what's happening in the moment with painful past experiences. These powerful sensations can take over completely, clouding our judgment and steering us right onto the rocks.*

David recommends you take a time out if you are not clear about what you are feeling before you go to a meeting that triggers all kinds of emotions. Write down the various words that describe what you are feeling. Broaden your vocabulary about emotions and find words that describe the underlying feelings.

Ask yourself, *I'm feeling frustrated; what is the cause?* Or, *I'm feeling supported; why?*
Or, *I'm feeling powerless; why is that?*

Getting in touch with your feelings can help clarify the reasons you are responding or reacting in a certain way.

Most of us have a limited vocabulary of feelings. And some try to categorize their emotions into two groups: positive and negative. If you perceive some of the emotions you experience as negative, you could limit the way you describe what's really going on.

⇔ ⇔ ⇔

Sweet and sour emotions

Here's a way to think about expanding your emotional vocabulary. Sweet and sour sauce is used to flavour all kinds of meals and desserts. An expression of emotions—the flavours in the conversation—can also be either sweet or sour, instead of negative or positive.

I have included a comprehensive list of sweet and sour emotions at the end of the book for your reference. The following ten *sweet* and ten *sour* words are not used enough. Experiment with these first and see how they enrich your vocabulary and the conversation when expressing emotions:

Sweet emotions

Encouraged. Reassured. Resilient. Inspired. Optimistic. Uplifted. Enlightened. Supported. Refreshed. Worthy.

Sour emotions

Discouraged. Perplexed. Alienated. Indecisive. Offended. Overwhelmed. Tormented. Powerless. Indifferent. Embarrassed.

Avoid using *sour* words such as confused, angry, useless, incompetent unless you know the person very well and have a high level of trust. Find alternative words for these emotions that are still true for you and won't cast you in an unfavourable light.

For example, instead of saying: *I'm feeling angry,* use another word such as *I'm feeling frustrated* or *disappointed*. And instead of saying, *I'm confused*, use an action word (the fourth anchor) instead; *I need more clarity about the next steps.*

Susan David says, *Emotionally agile people are dynamic. They demonstrate flexibility in dealing with our fast-changing, complex world. They tolerate high levels of stress and endure setbacks, while remaining engaged, open, and receptive.*

When you are mindful about what you are feeling, and convey it clearly in conversations, it's an expression of your truth. It helps to cut through the fog of internal politics, game-playing and the manipulation of power. Your authentic voice gives permission for your colleagues to use theirs.

Act—the fourth anchor

Once you have explored options and alternatives, resolved differences and understood each other's thinking and feelings about a topic, it's time for closure.

The fourth anchor is *Act*. A necessary conversation is not complete if it fades into a vague or unclear outcome. If it's a necessary conversation, it must end with an action. As Bushe puts it, being *descriptive* and *curious* are fundamental elements of clear leadership. When you lead a necessary conversation, you should:

- *describe* what you want;
- be *curious* about what the other person wants; and
- agree on a tangible action before the conversation ends.

You might think the outcome you want is obvious. Research (and my experience) has shown that the closure you want is not necessarily clear to your colleague. The closure or action your colleague agrees to must be included and acknowledged in the outcome.

Gervase Bushe observes, *you-language and we-language helps us to avoid responsibility for our opinions and judgments*. He's right: *We all want to make a difference* does not have the same resonance as *I would like you to use this agenda template at all our staff meetings*.

It's authentic and credible when you use *I* instead of *we* or *you*. When you say, *I am excited* or *I want you to take responsibility*, you take ownership of your thoughts, feelings and the actions you want.

Many people struggle with I-statements. Often, that's because they don't have a clear boundary line: a line in their mind that helps them be separate and not fused with the wants and feelings of others. Your boundary line helps you be self-aware and separate from your own feelings and thoughts so you can describe what you're observing, experiencing and what you want.

Dr. Henry Cloud says, *Knowing what I am to own and take responsibility for gives me freedom. Taking responsibility for my life opens up many different options.*

Two rules for every necessary conversation
Rule 1—Equal airtime

Describe your own experience using I-statements (not judgmental you-statements) and be curious. Allow time for insightful questions (it's not an interrogation).

When you strive for equal airtime between you and your colleague, the conversation has the potential to become a dialogue where each participant feels free to communicate using their authentic voice.

William Isaacs introduced the concept of psychological safety, a container or setting that enables conversations to be *a search for truth*. He says that for growth and new insights to flourish, three elements need to be part of every conversation: *energy, possibility and safety*.

These are signs of equal airtime—the natural rhythms of the ebb and flow in necessary conversations.

Equal airtime does not mean that your conversation has no time limits. Equal airtime means that within the time you have set aside for a necessary conversation—an hour for example—you're no longer just having a discussion, sharing information or trying to score points.

Equal airtime allows for moments of discovery, when you become open to new perspectives and thanks to William Isaacs, begin to not only solve problems, but *dissolve problems* together. He says we need to regain the *fire of conversation*, and further, *dialogue is a conversation in which people think together in relationship*.

I like the concept of dialogue—thinking together in relationship so that a problem is not only resolved, or solved but dissolved—transformed into a solution and no longer visible.

When you lead a necessary conversation, each participant or party should enjoy equal airtime. Listen with curiosity for underlying interests rather than judgment; park any reactions to the thoughts, feelings, wants and observations of the other person; ask clarifying questions, then check understanding. Describe your experience as honestly and authentically as you can so that others can understand. Use 'I' statements to take ownership of your own feelings and experience.

In practice:

Notice—*Describe* what you are noticing. Be *curious* about what the other person is noticing; or first be *curious* about what the other person is noticing, then *describe* what you are noticing.

I've noticed that in the past, we all had access to each other's calendars and then for the past three months, your calendar seems blocked. Are you aware of that, Maxine?

Think—*Describe* what you are thinking. Be *curious* about what the other person is thinking; or first be *curious* about what the other person is thinking, then *describe* what you are thinking.

I've been thinking that because we don't have access any more, staff are starting to wonder what's going on. In the absence of an explanation, soon they're going to make up stories.

Feel—*Describe* what you are feeling. Be *curious* about what the other person is feeling; or first be *curious* about what the other person is feeling, then *describe* what you are feeling.

I'm really concerned that sooner or later they will find out what's going on because people talk. Does that worry you as well?

Act—*Describe* what action you want. Be *curious* about what action the other person wants; or first be *curious* about what action the other person wants, then *describe* what action you want.

So how about we set up a time and I show you how to create your private calendar, and then restore the work calendar to open access?

As you use the anchors to navigate through a necessary conversation, remember to strive for equal airtime in the dialogue. Your objective should be a seamless mix of curiosity and authentic self-expression that stimulates the ebb and flow of dialogue.

Rule 2—Respectful and truthful

What does it mean to be respectful of the other person in the conversation?

It's being aware of and parking biases, such as religious, racial or cultural prejudice or assumptions you might have about the person you are talking with. And according to Isaacs, *thinking together implies you no longer take your own position as final*: you're open to making adjustments to your approach, point of view and the actions you will take or not take.

When you tolerate someone, your biases will leak out, no matter how hard you try to hide your pre-conceived assumptions of the other person. It means, for example, letting go of inauthentic civility and taking time to internally acknowledge and accept (not tolerate) someone who is LGTBQ or would like to be understood, be accepted and addressed as gender neutral.

The other person needs to feel safe when you are being truthful about what you've noticed and what you're thinking and feeling. Being truthful means you are clear and coherent with the words you use, taking care not to bruise the relationship.

When you're respectful and truthful, you step away from a positional perspective. Isaacs says it's the willingness to have *a conversation with a centre, not sides*.

Finding a way to integrate respect and truth is often a challenge. It involves talking about the elephant in the room - the undiscussables and undercurrents. When key issues are not swept under the carpet, they get the appropriate, unbiased attention and airtime they deserve in the centre of the conversation.

Being respectful and truthful are pillars of engagement, not an opportunity to take sides. Leaders who are respectful *and* truthful set a precedent for staff to emulate. Walking the talk builds morale and energizes the team; the principles of respect and truth are not concepts laminated on a wall as lofty values statements, but lived day to day.

Low and High Dialogue Leadership

A simple medical analogy involving levels of cholesterol helps illustrate the effects of poor and robust leadership communication.

LDL—or low density lipo-protein—is the sludge of bad cholesterol that clogs up people's veins and arteries, restricting the flow of blood and oxygen to the brain.

In an organizational or corporate setting, LDL represents *Low Dialogue Leadership*. In other words, in the absence of pro-active, clear communication, LDL happens. People make up stories to fill in the gaps. Repeated often enough, these stories become true for many employees, clogging up the *network of conversations* with alternative facts, delays, lack of clarity, and so on.

The downstream impacts are many: lower morale, a drop in standards, diminished pride, less initiative and motivation. And that can lead to higher employee turnover and a loss of key personnel with unique sets of knowledge and talent.

HDL—or high density lipo-protein—is the good cholesterol that clears the arteries so blood and oxygen can flow. HDL or *High Dialogue Leadership* is the only option for a leader where people need to work together and collaborate.

Zaffron and Logan, co-authors of *The Three Laws of Performance,* contend that an organization is its *network of conversations*. To build on this idea, an indicator of the vitality of employee engagement is the level *of HDL— High Dialogue Leadership*—that exists within an organization. When leaders are role models, their *HDL* is the spark that ignites authenticity, vulnerability and integrity in conversations.

High Dialogue Leadership is a fragile entity. Even when authenticity, vulnerability and integrity is the DNA of employee conversations, it can be snuffed out with a change of leadership that does not value authentic dialogue and necessary conversations as essential for getting results.

⇔ ⇔ ⇔

Microaggressions

Most people are unaware that their language and the way they come across can have a negative impact on people, with serious repercussions that can ripple through a workplace or relationships over time.

According to Wikipedia, a microaggression describes *behavioural or environmental indignities, whether intentional or unintentional, that communicate hostile, derogatory, or negative prejudicial slights and insults toward any group, particularly culturally marginalized groups.*

Examples of microaggressions—statements of irritation or insult

- ✧ I so enjoy talking to you; you're the whitest Black person I know.
- ✧ I know you live in Toronto, but where are you actually from?

- ⬥ I'm not sure if this will make you feel any better, but you don't look like you're gay.
- ⬥ Wow, you communicate well for an immigrant.
- ⬥ I'm blown away; you don't come across as transgender.
- ⬥ Cool, one of my colleagues at my work—Sam—he's also gay.

When someone has been microaggressive, either knowingly or unknowingly, it reveals biases—attitudes, stereotypes, and assumptions—that leave the person on the receiving end feeling insulted, irritated and uncomfortable.

Microaggressions cause psychological and mental pain: they diminish a person's sense of well-being and dignity through stereotypical discrimination.

Microaggressions are like a swarm of mosquitoes in the wilderness: they keep reminding the victim that they don't belong. And the longer they stay, the more painful it gets. The only way to get relief—albeit a wrong perception—is to back away and to give up something of oneself.

The authentic way to get relief is not to ignore it or back away but to address the microaggression. And the most appropriate way is to have a necessary conversation with that person.

⇔ ⇔ ⇔

Rut and river stories

It would be ideal if having necessary conversations was a seamless process. But things are not so simple. We all come to a conversation with a set of beliefs and stories. Our beliefs and the stories we tell ourselves define who we are and have an impact at work.

As a leader, you need to be able to identify and interrupt negative, de-energizing rut stories and encourage transformative river stories that lead to growth. So, what are rut and river stories?

Rut stories

Based on the teachings of Robert Hargrove, author and master coach, rut stories are often de-energizing, repetitive and defensive stories that people choose to tell about their experiences at work. People who tell rut stories might not be aware their stories are stuck in old ways of thinking and acting that produce no positive outcomes.

Their rut stories appeal to the fears, anxieties and frustrations of fellow workers. They plant stakes in the ground to protect territory and lean back to an idealised past.

Rut stories de-energise. They are cyclical and reinforce story endings that are filled with self-inflicted drama, office politics, hopelessness and disappointment. Some people who tell rut stories are so invested in their narrative, it can be a challenge for a leader to get them to give it up and nudge them to a different and more positive river story.

As a leader, be aware that rut stories can be compelling. You need to remain objective, park judgement and not allow yourself to get hooked into office dramas.

If you get drawn into a rut story and end up becoming emotionally invested in it, the perception of your objectivity as a leader will shift amongst staff. And not in a good way.

Examples of five classic rut stories

a. *Victim of the system*: this person always gets the raw deal and the payoff is attention, sympathy and support from others. They avoid taking ownership and responsibility and fear someone will get wise and uncover their game.

b. *Yes but*, or *I tried that*: each time a course of action is suggested, the response is *Yes but* or *I tried that* and then the person uses defensive reasoning why the suggestion won't work. The payoff is the same as playing a victim of the system, above. This person fears someone will challenge their defensive reasoning and stop paying attention to their cycle of despair.

c. *Can't say no*: this person justifies their story by insisting no one else is available, no one cares as much as they do and hints that no one is as experienced as they are. They imply they are uniquely qualified to do the job professionally and on time. The payoff is approval, being the go-to person for everything, admiration, accolades, being seen as professional and competent. It satisfies their need to be needed. This person fears that saying no will deflect the spotlight of attention.

d. *Impression management*: these types of stories position the storyteller as always being in control, extremely competent and eligible for promotion. The payoff is recognition, admiration, accolades, being seen as professional and competent. It satisfies a gnawing desire to be needed. This person fears being caught off guard and out of character.

e. *Don't rock the boat*: this person likes to game the system by staying below the radar, doing only what's required, playing strictly by the rules and not attracting attention. The payoff is job security, little stress, a comfortable routine and shirking responsibility. This person fears being called out for avoiding responsibility and not taking ownership.

The way to confront rut stories is through deep listening and insightful questions. Shine the light of enquiry over myth and superstition—rut stories at work—that have a veneer of credibility.

Defensive routines

According to Chris Argyris, a defensive routine is anything a group or individual does to avoid situations that are embarrassing and threatening. Defensive routines are often embedded in rut stories. With every defensive behaviour, there is a cost.

For example: a manager of the IT division uses a defensive routine to avoid talking about equal pay for women. He implies that the topic is undiscussable or off limits.

The result: employees eventually see through the avoidance and become convinced the manager is not being honest and is hiding something. And the cost? Rumours propagate at the speed of light, employees become suspicious of everything management does and management loses credibility.

Other examples of defensive routines involve creating smokescreens and distractions to resist learning, cover up issues and errors, protect turf, suppress alternate points of view, push one agenda to exclude others, blame others and bypass or minimize risks.

People who repeat a victim story build a watertight case using defensive reasoning about how people or the organization are doing them in. They wallow in victimhood and are very artful in getting people to support their cause.

It's so important that you challenge and interrupt defensive routines, rut stories and beliefs that appear to be generalizations and assumptions about people and processes not based on facts.

There is no one way to deal with people who use defensive routines and rut stories to their advantage. The first step is to recognize what's going on and then to address the behaviours, either as a feedback conversation or as a necessary conversation - or both.

River stories

Every rut story needs to be replaced with an energising river story that nudges the culture away from pessimism and defeat to optimism, engagement and purpose.

Rivers find the path of least resistance over millennia and carve out a way through the environment to the sea. Looking down from the International Space Station, you might not be able to distinguish between a rut and a river until a sliver of water is reflected in the sun.

River stories that welcome diversity, spark innovation and are purposeful take time to carve their way into the minds and hearts of employees. But when they do, they become the meaning that drives momentum at work.

Telling river stories at work can inspire and elevate the human spirit. That does not mean we create an illusion that masks reality. River stories help us embrace our situation without downplaying actual challenges and problems.

People who tell river stories are perceived as inspiring, authentic, transparent and come across without a hidden agenda. They tend to energise the culture at work for positive change, speaking of possibility and a transformational future.

You can help your colleagues recognise rut stories and defensive routines and shift to river stories that are transformative and lead to growth.

When you hear a rut story, you need to name it. Explain to your colleague or learning partner what a rut story or defensive routine is to help them see things from a new and different perspective.
One way to do this is to engage your colleague in a series of insightful questions that will help interrupt the rut story and pattern of defensiveness.

Example of a necessary conversation between Acey and Rob:

Rob, from what you've just told me, and I could be wrong, it seems as if you come across as doing what's required—the minimum—to get by and nothing more. That's my perception; how do you see your role?

And if Rob decides to disclose more information that confirms what Acey noticed, further insightful questions can be asked such as: *How is that working for you?* And *What's the pay-off?*

⇔ ⇔ ⇔

Recognize personality preferences

Many organizations have sent their employees on training courses that attempt to help them better understand their own natural tendencies and personality preferences and those of their colleagues.

The concept of categorizing personality preferences is based on years of work by various researchers and psychologists. These indicators are designed to interpret and explain individual psychological style in the workplace—the way people show up.
Some of the personality style indicator programs claim to offer a wide range of insights, yet lack peer-reviewed scientific validation.

According to Oldham and Morris, *Your personality style is your organizing principle. It propels you on your life path. It represents the orderly arrangement of all your attributes, thoughts, feelings, attitudes, behaviors, and coping mechanisms. It is the distinctive pattern of your psychological functioning—the way you think, feel, and behave—that makes you definitely you.*

While no one can be defined only by colour or label (we're all blends to varying degrees), each indicator—a colour or label—is associated with certain personality traits or behaviours.

The belief is that with increased understanding of ourselves and others, that deeper communication will occur and conflict will decrease.

As you understand your own and others' personality preferences and behavioural styles, you learn how to better engage with your co-workers.

When you prepare to have a necessary conversation, reflect on your own and the personality preference of the other person. This will help you to more effectively engage with them and reach an outcome you both want.

⇔ ⇔ ⇔

The 10-point necessary conversation checklist
Before you have the conversation

1. Purpose - what outcome do you want from this necessary or crucial conversation?
2. Have you clearly communicated the reason for the conversation in neutral terms and the venue? Sometimes it's a good idea to meet off-site to help to remove unnecessary power differentials and create a sense of safety and privacy.
3. What are your perceptions and assumptions and what are your colleague's perceptions and assumptions?
4. What are your colleague's personality preferences? What are your preferences?
5. What unintended messages should you be mindful of when you communicate?

During the conversation

6. Remember the two rules: equal airtime and be respectful and truthful.
7. If the subject is sensitive, remember to ask permission before speaking about what you've noticed or are thinking and always ask for their perspective.
8. Use each anchor point (Notice, Think, Feel, Act) as part of your dialogue by asking insightful questions and sharing your experiences and observations.
9. Jointly agree on the action if possible and ensure it is clear—who will do what by when.
10. Ensure the outcome or agreed action is documented. Ask your colleague to email the agreed action to you. Or if you are having a necessary conversation with a colleague, customer or your boss, offer to send an email detailing what was agreed.

Necessary Conversation Example 3—Katia and Pendra

Katia has worked for the past five years at a university in the International Student Services area. She's a recruitment advisor, responsible for attracting students from other countries to study and obtain a degree at the university. She is one of a team of six recruiters who reports to Pendra.

With her considerable experience travelling to other countries to meet with prospective students and promote the university's offerings, Katia knows she has some important insights on opportunities to increase interest and enrollment. She loves her job but has become increasingly frustrated by Pendra's continued resistance to her ideas to grow and improve the program. It seems every time she suggests a different approach or innovative idea, Pendra does not hear what she's saying or shuts her down.

Although she considers herself an engaged and contributing team member, lately Katia has noticed she's feeling less motivated and excited about her work. She's showing up and doing her job, but her enthusiasm for going above and beyond has waned. She's started thinking about looking for other work where her creative energy might be more appreciated. Katia has decided that she needs to have a necessary conversation with Pendra first, to let him know how significantly his lack of support and encouragement has affected her.

Katia makes an appointment to meet with Pendra; she lets him know in advance it concerns a personal matter. They meet at a coffee shop near the university campus.

"So, Katia, you wanted to talk to me about a personal matter? What's going on?"

Yes, Pendra, thanks for making time for us to meet. I'd like to discuss my role and your expectations.

"Your role as a recruitment advisor? What's not clear about it?"

Well, my understanding as far as the job description goes is to source potential applicants from other countries who may benefit from attending the university. That involves research, travel, and identifying key relationships. How do you see my role and the job description?

"Those are the basics, yes."

I try to go above and beyond the basics. I really like the work, Pendra. I see many opportunities to improve our efforts in recruiting international students. Can I share with you what I've noticed? These are my perceptions and I'd like to get your perspective.

"Go ahead."

NOTICE—*You see, Pendra, I have presented lots of those ideas to you over this last year, but it seems every time I bring up an idea—and this is my perception—you don't seem to pay attention to what I'm saying. You usually say we'll discuss it later. And later never happens.*

"I don't know what you mean. I welcome your ideas. Sometimes, though, you bring them up in a staff meeting and we have lots of items on the agenda so it's just not feasible to discuss them at that time."

FEEL—*I get that, but you never approach me afterwards to pick up the conversation, Pendra. I'm left wondering if you thought it was a bad idea, or if you've forgotten. It's frustrating. And I need to let you know I am disappointed. I'm losing some of my mojo because I don't feel I'm being heard.*

"You're losing your mojo. Okay, I can see that what I'm doing or not doing is affecting you, Katia."

THINK—*And we seldom have one-on-one meetings, Pendra, where the two of us can discuss my performance and many ideas I have for enhancing the department's efforts. What are your thoughts on where I'm coming from?*

"I'm realising I've got to do some things differently. But what's worrying me now is I'm trying to think of a time when I shut you down, when you didn't feel heard."

NOTICE—*Can I remind you about something that happened recently, Pendra? I don't want this to come across as if I'm taking notes of every time we talk, which I'm not.*

"You have the floor."

Well, a few weeks back I approached you about the university's website. Our department has very little presence on the site, and I know we could do a better job of describing and promoting what's available and why an international student might want to study here.

"I vaguely remember that. It's been a busy month."

That's exactly it, Pendra. I know you've been busy. We're all busy. What I told you then was our website is the first place people go to check us out. We have so little relevant information there that I fear international students will equate that with the type of education they'd get here. Anyhow, I have lots of ideas on improvements to the site and I mentioned my concerns to you and you didn't seem interested at all.

"I had concerns about budget and resources to do this."

FEEL—*I understand that, but I was disappointed you didn't sit down with me and talk through about what could be done. I was thinking some small copy changes that I could make. I just wanted a chance to discuss it.*

"My job is to manage the budget and ensure everyone's focused on recruitment. No one has the time in the foreseeable future to be working on anything but hitting our recruitment goals. But I hear you."

I'm glad you're hearing me. And please don't take this wrong, Pendra. How do you feel about upgrading the website to attract more international students?

"The first thing that concerns me is budget, Katia. We're a university and as you know, we're always stretched on finances. And the second thing is I worry about is that you'll burn yourself out adding this to your job."

Maybe we can discuss the details later, Pendra. This is just one example of an idea I've presented to you and when I don't sense you're open to them, I feel demotivated.

"Ok, I hear what you're saying. I didn't know you felt that way. I apologize for coming across as preoccupied. What can we do going forward?"

Well, I know your day is packed full. And having to work in an environment of no budget must be frustrating.

"That a pretty accurate assessment."

ACT—*So here's what I'd like to see going forward. I would like to have regular meetings with you where we discuss my role, my performance and my ideas. And I would like to know you've heard me, Pendra. Is that okay?*

"Totally okay and I agree. I'll set up a meeting once every two weeks with you for one hour. We can start with that and check in with each other to see if it's working for both of us. I'll ask Patty to put those dates in my calendar for the year and to make sure our meetings don't get bumped off. Does that sound okay, Katia?"

Let's do that, Pendra. I really appreciate you taking the time to hear me out.

"You're welcome. I'm glad we had this conversation and I apologize for being a bit defensive at first."

Now that you've read the conversation, please review the four anchors that Katia used to guide the conversation to a successful outcome. Take note that the conversation can go back and forth between the conversational anchors.

⇔ ⇔ ⇔

Ten potential necessary conversations

Here are ten examples of necessary conversations that might trigger ideas for conversations that you need to have in your workplace.

1. Your manager's choice of a new hire bothers you

Today is Friday and after a full day of interviews, your manager says to you: "Well, there's no contest. Any reasonable person can see that the first person we interviewed this morning is the best person for the job. Don't you agree?"

You don't agree but say nothing. You have serious reservations about the selection of this person for the job. You know your team better than your manager and your gut instinct tells you this will not be a good fit. You also know that the person your manager is recommending, is related to one of your manager's golfing partners.

You think about this on the weekend. Today is Monday and you decide to have a necessary conversation with your manager to express your reservations about hiring this person.

2. Your summer vacation and the project launch

You have been working on a project for the last two years. The project is in its final stages and will go live this September. Your family has been pressuring you to take a break—they have been complaining they hardly ever see you anymore.

On Sunday, one of your few days off, you book airline and hotel tickets to take your family to Disneyland for a two-week summer vacation. This is a surprise for your family. After all, the project is on track.

The next day is Monday and your manager says to you: "As you know, the project you have been working on for the last two years is going live on September 30. You are the only one I can trust to continue managing it during the summer. I hope you don't mind not taking vacation this summer; we'll make it up for you big time later."

You need to have a necessary conversation with your manager to reach some sort of compromise.

3. Your colleague uses up all the airtime at meetings

You and your colleague both co-chair working group sessions that mentor innovators within your organization.

Your colleague has worked at the organization for 16 years. Most of the innovators who attend these sessions are millennials who have been on staff for less than three years. The purpose of these working group sessions is to encourage innovators to bring their ideas from concept to delivery.

You have become increasingly frustrated because your colleague tends to use up all the airtime when providing feedback to the innovators. Some are showing signs that they will withdraw from the sessions because they don't get a chance to share their ideas and don't feel heard.

You need to have a necessary conversation with your colleague to get this sorted out.

4. Your boss is going to retire soon

Your manager has been with the organization for 38 years and will retire two years from now. You have been with the organization for four years. You can see so many missed opportunities and are eager to make a difference. At the same time, you are frustrated with the slow pace of change: everyone knows that your manager doesn't want to rock the boat before he/she retires.

You have a great idea that can make a positive impact and save some serious money for the organization over the next 10 years.

You need to have a necessary conversation with your manager to initiate a change.

5. Your colleague is missing deadlines

Five of you are working on a high-impact project for your organization. Senior management are aware of the risk and potential benefits and are very supportive of your team and the project. Each bi-weekly progress report helps to secure support and funding for the project.

Your colleague is responsible for these reports but the last three have been late. As a result, you are aware of some unease amongst the management team. If this continues, they might get the wrong impression and question the value of the project.

You would be extremely disappointed if this happened and would not get the opportunity to work on an exciting project from start to completion. And you would not be able to list this high-profile project on your CV.

You need to have a necessary conversation with your colleague to address this issue.

6. Your colleague is becoming increasingly negative

You have noticed that over the period of a year, your colleague who used to be enthusiastic about new ideas, innovation and taking on challenges, has become increasingly negative at your team meetings. As the team leader, it worries you that this negativity is starting to impact other members of your team. Some people are now adopting a *glass half-empty* view of things and others are avoiding this person.

You need to have a necessary conversation with this employee to address this issue.

7. The disrespectful colleague

One of the members of your team has an energizing, extroverted personality. This employee is liked by staff and comes across as the joker of the group. It bothers you that this colleague, while popular, shows respect to certain groups but behind the scenes, mocks and insults them. These jokes are often about religion, members of the LGBTQ community and are often tinged with subtle racism.

You need to have a necessary conversation with this employee to address this issue.

8. The introverted colleague

You want to encourage someone who reports to you to take ownership of a new initiative that will be extremely challenging but also rewarding within a few years. You know this person is quiet, shy, introverted, and risk-averse yet extremely bright and talented. You see great potential in this person and know it will be a massive confidence-booster and more secure career path if he/she takes it on.

You need to have a necessary conversation with your colleague to persuade him/her to take on this project. You know from experience that if you come on too strong, you might get compliance but not commitment.

9. The new manager comes across as micro-aggressive

Your new manager has only been in the position for three weeks and already you and your team are experiencing the impacts of the way she communicates.

She is unaware of the way she comes across. She recently told one of your colleagues that *he communicates well for an immigrant*. And then a few days later, she said she knows Travis is gay but he's *welcome in the department*.

The statements she makes about people is having an impact on everyone: morale is falling and people are starting to feel insulted and judged.

You need to have a necessary conversation with your manager to address this issue.

10. The new hire is not delivering results

Your unit is under pressure to go live on a large project in the next three months. You are short-staffed—down to a team of five. You need more skilled people to complete the project on time and within budget. You have asked HR to help. They sent you a new hire from another area to help out. The new hire has a PhD in the subject area but no relevant work experience. The result: the new hire spends valuable time analyzing and providing theoretical arguments for different approaches to the project but is not delivering any tangible results. Your team is getting more stressed out as they continue to work long hours while this person seems oblivious to the team effort required to complete the project.

You need to have a necessary conversation with this person to address this issue.

⇔ ⇔ ⇔

The Six Leadership Conversations

Dene Rossouw

The Tough Conversation

The Tough Conversation
List of topics in this chapter

- ✧ When to use *The Tough Conversation*
- ✧ *The Tough Conversation*—introducing Natalia and Serge (to be continued)
- ✧ The high cost of avoiding tough conversations
- ✧ Reframing
- ✧ Gauging the emotional temperature
- ✧ Clarifying the issues, your interests and approach
- ✧ Communicating the reason for the conversation and the expected results
- ✧ *The Tough Conversation* using LEAD
- ✧ *The Tough Conversation* example—Natalia and Serge using LEAD
- ✧ Thoughts about *The Tough Conversation* Natalia had with Serge
- ✧ Notes to help you navigate tough conversations
  - o Compromise, collaboration, cooperation
  - o What to do when issues appear to be polarized and emotive
  - o Power imbalances – Power-Over and Power-Less
  - o Authentic personal power
  - o Preparing for your Tough Conversation
  - o Three examples of issues that require tough conversations

When entrenched conflict and misunderstandings are at the heart of issues at work, *The Tough Conversation* is a measured and structured approach to help you resolve the issues.

The Tough Conversation is the fifth leadership conversation. It is a dialogue of conflict resolution built around four conversational anchors using the mnemonic LEAD:

- ✧ L—Lay out. Lead. Listen.
- ✧ E—Explore. Express. Explain.
- ✧ A—Agree. Acknowledge. Ask.
- ✧ D—Decide. Detail. Document.

When to use *The Tough Conversation*

The Tough Conversation helps you have a structured conversation and document a course of action to resolve misunderstandings, deal with conflict and entrenched behaviours that cause disruption and deplete morale at work. It is another essential tool for your leadership toolbox.

helps you have a structured conversation and document a course of action to resolve misunderstandings, deal with conflict and entrenched behaviours that cause disruption and deplete morale at work

Use *The Tough Conversation* after having at least two *Necessary Conversations* if behaviours haven't changed or commitments didn't lead to action.

The Tough Conversation—introducing Natalia and Serge

Natalia works for a company in Vancouver that builds waterparks for clients in 25 countries around the world. She's recently been asked to take over the management of the design department. Each person in her department—there are 20 staff—is responsible for various aspects of the design of the waterparks.

One of the members of her team—Serge—has an energetic, extroverted personality. Serge is liked by staff and comes across as the joker of the group. It bothers her that while Serge gets along well with everyone, behind the scenes, he mocks and insults certain groups of people. His jokes are often about religion or members of the LGBTQ community. Natalia has noticed many of his jokes are tinged with subtle racism.

Within the first month of taking over as manager, at least five people approached her about Serge. Natalia immediately made an appointment with Serge and had a *Necessary Conversation* with him.
Serge downplayed the issue and told Natalia that where he comes from, it's no big deal, everyone does it. He said his colleagues needed to chill and shouldn't take life so seriously.

Serge reluctantly agreed, though, to be more self aware of how his words and beliefs could hurt and alienate colleagues.

Now, three months later, Natalia hasn't noticed any real change and staff are still coming to her. Natalia sets up a time to have a *Tough Conversation* with Serge. She positions it in an email to Serge as a follow-up to their previous conversation.

To be continued . . .

⇔ ⇔ ⇔

The high cost of avoiding tough conversations

If managers have a habit of avoiding the discomfort of tough conversations to resolve an issue, it sets a precedent for a culture of conflict avoidance.

This results in, as Liane Davey, a New York Times Bestselling author puts it—an accumulation of conflict debt—*the sum of all undiscussed and unresolved issues that stand in the way of progress.*

These undiscussed and unresolved issues are measurable psychological and productivity costs that mount up over time and manifest as lower morale, increased turnover of staff, lack of incentive, minimal innovation and more.

It takes time, even years, to replace a toxic culture with one that is authentic, open and engaging—a culture where all employees feel valued, where conflict is not avoided and where everyone feels comfortable speaking their truth without fear of retribution.

⇔ ⇔ ⇔

Reframing

Rephrasing and reframing of key elements of a tough conversation is an important empathic response and should never be a dispassionate clinical process.

It aligns with the first conversation, *The Listening Conversation*: to listen for and summarise your understanding of the other person's whys. Then rephrase and reframe their key whys or interests—to check for understanding—before asking if they would be willing to hear your point of view.

Within most organizations, certain individuals have a tendency to:
- See things as black and white
- Dehumanize other groups and their points of view
- Reduce issues down to over-simplistic beliefs about their colleagues including the factors that have contributed to the dispute.

James Hollis, the Jungian analyst and author, echoes the danger of simplistic beliefs noting that fundamentalism is an *anxiety management system that finesses the nuances of doubt and ambiguity through rigid and simplistic belief systems.*

Anatol Rapoport, an American mathematical psychologist and founder of the Mental Health Research Institute (MHRI) at the University of Michigan said that when dealing with people who have simplistic and different beliefs from you, rephrase and reframe their beliefs and the key components about what drives them. Then ask if they would be open to hear your perspective.

Everyone has a responsibility to build social capital—trust, lived values, authentic relationships—by appreciating healthy differences and encouraging diverse points of view. It includes interrupting and correcting misperceptions and characterizations of colleagues (and members of the public) that undermine the social fabric and pollute espoused values of the workplace.

Margaret Heffernan, CEO, writer and keynote speaker, says that you should view a colleague who has a different point of view as a thinking partner instead of an enemy or potential source of conflict. She says, *we have to resist the neurobiological drive, which means that we really prefer people mostly like ourselves, and it means we have to seek out people with different backgrounds, different disciplines, different ways of thinking and different experiences, and find ways to engage with them.*

She views conflict, when it does happen, as constructive if the social capital and relationships at work are robust enough to support candour: dialogue without damage.

According to Heffernan, when authentic relationships of trust have been built up over time—like a habit of consistent investing—an organization's social capital *compounds even as we spend it.*

⇔ ⇔ ⇔

Gauging the emotional temperature

When I described *The Necessary Conversation*, you will recall that the third anchor of a necessary conversation is *feelings*—to share what you are feeling in the moment and to ask what the other person is feeling.

If the person you are talking to says they are *concerned* and you respond by saying, *tell me more*, other layers of emotions such as *frustration or disappointment* might come into the conversation. These feeling words help surface the truth of what's really going on.

When you decide a tough conversation is needed, it's because things have been building up over time and need to be addressed. It's so important to uncover the layers of emotions (what's driving my anger?) so you can honestly share what you're feeling and not conceal your emotions. If you don't identify the layers of feeling—disappointment and frustration leading to anger—micro-indicators of your emotions will leak out anyhow. The other person in the conversation will most often misinterpret these signals and make up their own story about what you're feeling.

It's far better to identify the layers of emotions you are experiencing and explain that you are feeling disappointed or disillusioned or frustrated, rather than just saying you're angry. Then add your own reasons or whys such as your expectations were dashed or commitments were not kept.

When you read about *The Necessary Conversations,* you will remember that feelings were placed in two bowls—sweet and sour—to help you widen your feelings vocabulary (your emotional agility) and help articulate more accurately what's really going on.

Clifford N. Lazarus, Ph.D, a licensed psychologist and co-founder of *The Lazarus Institute,* suggests it helps to gauge the temperature of your emotion using a thermometer with a Celsius scale: 100 degrees is the steam point for emotions (they can be sweet or sour) while zero is super cool, everything is fine. If you are feeling optimistic and hopeful, gauge the temperature: is it 50° or 60° or 75° (on the warm side)? If you are not feeling cynical or wary, what's the temperature: 20° or 30° or 35° (on the cooler side)?

When you are about to have a tough conversation, take your emotional temperature and find appropriate words to describe what you are feeling.

Clarify the issues, your interests and approach

A tough conversation is needed when you have had at least two *Necessary Conversations* with a colleague about an issue or problem and no satisfactory changes in behaviour or outcome are evident.

When you prepare for a tough conversation, it helps to think through the issues, your approach and your interests - or whys. Examples of issues—an escalation from a necessary conversation to a tough conversations could be:

- Disrespect for a colleague
- Bullying a colleague
- Not delivering on commitments
- Manipulation of processes to benefit certain groups
- A passive aggressive attitude
- A serious disregard for customer service standards

It's important to clarify that everyone is talking about the same issue. When you feel strongly about an issue, you will usually take up a position or point of view about it.

Try to reframe your point of view as an approach rather than a position that's cast in stone. The person or people you are dealing with will also take up a position. Depending on their situation, they could be heavily invested in their position or remain flexible.

If you spend time clarifying everyone's position up front, it makes resolution more difficult because positions become entrenched and ultimatums get baked in.

Instead of clarifying everyone's position, begin an explorative enquiry into what's important to them and share what's important to you. These are the whys or interests that everyone holds dear. If you stick at it, you will find common ground—shared interests that point to a glimpse of a solution.

Once you have sufficient common interests, they become the building blocks of an inside-out approach. The shared interests, concerns and whys help to a resolve a tough situation.

If you always default to some form of compromise to accommodate someone, it can erode your personal power and reduce your effectiveness.

If you adopt an inside-out approach, you will have more success at resolving issues because you work towards a resolution from the centre of a tough conversation: the real interest and whys.

Resolving a tough conversation requires a level of trust and authentic engagement that is creative, a solution that is not pre-determined. You end up with more clarity about the issues and a broader consensus of common interests that leads to better resolutions of tough conversations.

⇔⇔⇔

Communicate the reason for the conversation and the expected results

One of the first things you need to do is let the person know you would like to meet with them to talk and why. If you can do this in person, so much the better.

If not, send an email with a clear, neutral reason for meeting.

That's one of the things you need to get right. What do you want to talk about? You need to communicate two things in a non-judgmental and neutral way up front: the *Reason* for the conversation and the *Result* you want going forward.

When you let a colleague or employee know in advance the *Reason* for the conversation and the *Result* you want, it gives them time to prepare. What you should not do is send a vague, ambiguous email—with no clear reason what you want to talk about—to an employee or colleague on a Friday afternoon, for example, requesting a meeting on the Monday. This will send their stress levels through the roof as they speculate all weekend about the meeting.

⇔⇔⇔

The Tough Conversation using LEAD

The LEAD process consists of four anchors to help you navigate through a *Tough Conversation*. Each anchor has three key words that guide you through the conversation so that you don't come across as scripted. It's important that you use the anchors and key words as a guide so that your conversation has a structure and direction. At the same time, allow your personality to come across: you need to feel comfortable and authentic, even though you are having a tough conversation.

L—Lay out. Lead. Listen.

Lay out the reasons for the conversation, including impacts of the behaviour.

Lead the conversation in a neutral way based on facts.

Listen for new information. Park judgment.

E—Explore. Express. Explain.

Explore the interests (or whys) of your colleague and summarise what's important to them.

Express what's important to you—your own interests (or whys).

Explain the benefits of finding a solution.

A—Agree. Acknowledge. Ask.

Agree on common interests that are shared and important to them and you.

Acknowledge differences, especially interests that are not shared in common.

Ask for their commitment to a creative solution.

D—Decide. Detail. Document.

Decide on a way forward based on shared interests.

Detail the next steps. Highlight joint responsibilities.

Document the action. Ensure your colleague has a copy of the action.

⇔⇔⇔

Let's go back to the *Tough Conversation* Natalia needs to have with Serge.

The Tough Conversation between Natalia and Serge using LEAD

Natalia sets aside an hour to prepare for her *Tough Conversation* with Serge the next day.

She jots down some notes of what she needs to be mindful of:

1. ## The reason for the conversation and expected result

   I should clarify for myself and communicate with Serge in advance about the *Reason* we need to meet: I'd like to follow up on our previous conversation about the way his behaviour is being perceived by his colleagues.

   And the expected *Result*: I want him to be mindful of what he says and how it impacts his colleagues. I would like him to commit to communicating in a way that builds relationships and to not tell stories or jokes anymore about any person or group. He is free to tell self-deprecating stories about his own experience.

2. ## Perspectives

   My point of view is Serge has not made any changes and his attitude and behaviour is unsettling and comes across as judgmental to his colleagues.

   His point of view could be that he's tried and no-one's mentioned anything to him and he means no harm. Therefore, it's no big deal.

3. ## Model the behaviours

   I need to have the conversation with Serge and not avoid it. I'm hopeful that staff will notice that I am addressing it, whatever the outcome. It's important for me to model the behaviours and come out, as it were, for all staff so everyone feels accepted, no matter their background, culture, religion, gender and physical ability.

4. ## Mindset of curiosity

   It's important for me to stay curious throughout the conversation. I can't engage Serge if I have a fixed mindset about what Serge has or has not done. If I have a fixed mindset, I will search for evidence to confirm my point of view—a confirmation bias. I also need to be mindful of not labeling any behaviour as a judgment, because he could interpret this as a character flaw or a destiny without hope of change. Instead, I need to be open-minded and curious.

5. **Respectful truthfulness**

   It's important I respectfully hear what Serge is saying (and not saying) and make him feel validated for the good work he is doing, without tiptoeing around the issue: mocking LGBTQ and religious people and staff behind their backs. He needs to know I've heard and tried to understand where he is coming from yet I'm being truthful about addressing the issues.

6. **Empathy and self-empathy**

   Empathize with Serge and try to see things from his perspective: Emotion—he could feel embarrassed, defensive, indignant, apologetic. I anticipate he'll first feel indignant that I'm bringing this up again and later he could feel embarrassed. It means he has to make real, measurable changes to his behaviour as there will be consequences for inaction.
   When I think about where I'm coming from:
   Emotion—I'm feeling divided—wary that this could blow up into something bigger but also cautiously optimistic that it can be resolved.
   It means I am taking the appropriate steps, however uncomfortable and building my confidence as a manager to have these conversations sooner than later.

7. **Anticipating the future**

    If I don't address these behaviours with Serge, I anticipate costs to our team such as lower morale and productivity and potential loss of key staff. I think it can lead to conflict with staff if it's not addressed. At the moment, I see it as a productive tough conversation, not conflict. I also hope for a growth-oriented and positive outcome.

⇔ ⇔ ⇔

Tough Conversation Example 1—Natalia and Serge (continued)

A few days before Natalia met with Serge, she sent him an email explaining the *Reason* for the conversation and the *Result* or outcome she expected:

Serge, I'd like to follow up on our previous conversation about the way you come across to our colleagues. I want to set up a time with you to discuss this. I'm hoping that at the end of our conversation, you will be more mindful of what you say, how it impacts your colleagues and find a way to express yourself that builds relationships.

Two days later, Serge and Natalia meet in a local coffee shop off-site.

L—Lay out. Lead. Listen.

Lay out the reasons for the conversation, including impacts of the behaviour.
Lead the conversation in a neutral way based on facts.
Listen for new information. Park judgment.

Hi Serge, thanks for making the time to talk. Before we get going, I'd like to assure you that what we discuss remains confidential between us.

"Sounds so serious, Natalia. And confidential, hey? You mean I can't tell everyone in the office? Only joking."

That's right, Serge, both of us need to keep what we discuss confidential. Is that okay?

"Whatever. But okay."

I'd like to follow up on our previous discussion we had three months ago. What is your understanding of the outcome of that conversation? Remember, you emailed it to me.

"I've always told jokes, Natalia. My jokes are harmless. People get to laugh and that's a good thing."

I'd like to talk about jokes and what energizes you in a moment, Serge, but for now, remind me of what you agreed to do three months ago.

"You don't let up, do you? I feel like you're like a dog with a bone, sorry for the analogy."

I have it here in front of me but I'd prefer it if you own it, Serge, what you agreed.

"Okay. I said I wouldn't tell jokes that might offend, or mock anyone, especially members of the LGBTQ community."

And . . .

"I would not tell any story or joke that, how do you say it, discriminates against another person or group."

And where?

"In their presence or behind people's backs."

That's it. So, Serge, here's the context. It's been three months since we last spoke. I'm still hearing from your colleagues that not much has changed. Everyone who has spoken to me has also brought it up with you. It's an important issue, Serge. I'd like us to talk about it.

"I don't remember anyone talking to me about it. If I can't remember them talking to me, it can't be a big deal."

It is a big deal, Serge. It's an important issue that we need to talk through—for me and the well-being of the team. I'm curious why you think mocking someone—calling them a faggot—is okay?

"It's a joke—everyone gets it, just a joke."

E—Explore. Express. Explain.

Explore the interests (or whys) of your colleague and summarise what's important to them.
Express what's important to you—your own interests (or whys).
Explain the benefits of finding a solution.

You have a different perspective on this than I do, Serge. My approach is always about not harming or hurting anyone, even inadvertently. Give me some background as to why—you've mentioned it many times—you think it's no big deal?

"As you know, I'm from a small village in Eastern Europe. Where I come from, you say it like it is and if someone gets upset, too bad. That's how we communicate. That's how I grew up, you get respect by letting people know where you stand. And when I went into the military, you get to the point, no messing around. If it's a joke about a homo, no one takes offence. Everyone laughs. They love it where I come from. They always asked me to carry on. Even here in our office, people ask me to tell them another story."

From what you've said, Serge, it sounds like telling stories is important for you?

"Yup, stories and jokes are what I do. It's a big stress reliever for me here at work."

That's interesting, that you tell stories and jokes to relieve stress. Can I share with you where I'm coming from?

"Go ahead."

If I understand your perspective, telling jokes is no big deal because you mean no harm to anyone. And it's a stress reliever.

"Correct."

Okay, from my perspective, when I hear you talk about someone—even jokingly—in a demeaning way, I become concerned. I know you don't mean harm to any person or group, but everyone in our team most probably knows someone who you are making fun of.

"I never thought of that."

So, for example Serge, I have a gay son. Marie-Anne has an autistic daughter. When you make jokes about homos or retards, it cuts to the core of our people because they interpret it that you are making fun of their loved ones. My son has to face a lot of willful ignorance and discrimination for who he is.

"Whaaat?"

And Marie-Anne's daughter can play just about any music on the piano – from jazz to rock. But you can't engage her in a conversation because the way she processes information is different from you and me. It hurts Marie-Anne when you make jokes using the term "retards."

"Jeeez, Natalia. I never knew this. Why didn't someone tell me?"

They did try, Serge. But I guess you were in a different space. And I think—I could be wrong on this—you carried a badge of honour that was part of your background, to tell jokes and have fun. There's nothing wrong with jokes, and we can talk more about that another time.

Do you see the importance of finding another way to communicate?

"I sure do, Natalia."

A—Agree. Acknowledge. Ask.

Agree on common interests that are shared and important to them and you.
Acknowledge differences, especially interests that are not shared in common between you.
Ask for their commitment to a creative solution.

From what I've heard you say, Serge, and I believe this about you, you have no desire to hurt anyone?

"I feel so bad now. I didn't mean to hurt anyone."

I know that was not your intent, Serge. But you need to realize that certain stories and jokes have an enormous impact on people. I felt very uncomfortable when I realized you were carrying on as usual and not aware of the impact of your stories. Yet I was also cautiously optimistic that you would receive it in a good way and commit to make changes to the way you show up. I don't want this to suppress your natural ability to energize people. But it must happen in a way that does not harm anyone.

I want to focus on next steps, Serge. How open are you to trying a different approach?

"For sure."

D—Decide. Detail. Document.

Decide on a way forward based on shared interests.
Detail the next steps. Highlight joint responsibilities.
Document the agreed action. Get your colleague to write up and send you the agreed action.

I think we're very close now, Serge, in that we both see the value of stories: stories that don't bruise people in terms of their culture or beliefs but instead build relationships, stories that inspire and motivate others.

"I've been using this style of humour for so long, it's going to be a steep learning curve for me. I need to figure out how to do that, you know."

We can talk more about this in more detail later, Serge, but a safer way to go is to talk about your own challenges, more of a self-deprecating humour. Every successful comedian knows that's the safest and most authentic way to go. People identify with your struggles and it can be inspirational and motivational.

"I'm willing to give it a try, Natalia. It's a bit of a relief. I thought you were going to fire me."

Not at all, Serge. But it did concern me that there could be legal challenges for you if someone interpreted your jokes in a personal way, as if you were mocking them or their family.
So, what will you make a point of doing differently going forward?

"Well, I'm going to be super mindful of what I say and how it impacts my colleagues. And I think, also outside of work. It's been a real eye-opener for me. I realize I've not taken our first conversation seriously. So, my apologies, Natalia."

Apology accepted, Serge. I'd like to challenge you with an assignment.

"Okay. I'm listening."

I'd like you to adopt a new badge of honour, one of mutual respect and curiosity about where your colleagues are coming from and what's important to them. So, tomorrow I'm introducing a new feedback approach called From Growth to Great to a few members of our team. I'd like you to join the group. We're going to learn how to ask for feedback from colleagues and supervisors. It's at 10am in the training room.

"I'll be there."

Great. This is our pilot group and eventually everyone in the department will learn how to ask and provide feedback to each other. After the session, everyone in the group, including you, will be tasked with asking for feedback from four of your colleagues.

"So everyone will be going through the training?"

All staff, including me. Based on the feedback received, everyone will be expected to develop an action plan. We're going to be doing the From Growth to Great feedback exercise every six months.

"Sounds interesting."

It will be very interesting and insightful, Serge. Now, to wrap up. What I've understood as we've been speaking is that you're going to be super mindful of what you say in future and how it impacts your colleagues. And you're going to find a way to express yourself, maybe by telling self-deprecating stories of your own life that builds instead of breaks down relationships. Have I summed it up correctly?

"That sums it clearly, Natalia. I've got it."

Great. I'd like you to send me an email, before you attend the session tomorrow, that reflects your understanding of what you've agreed to and what you need to pay attention to going forward.

"Ok, Natalia, I'll get to it today. Thanks for making the time to speak with me. It's been very insightful. I'm looking forward to putting on a new badge of honour."

⇔ ⇔ ⇔

Thoughts about *The Tough Conversation* Natalia had with Serge

The reasons for having a tough conversation are varied. But the common thread is the build-up of stress and anxiety by staff when opportunities for addressing issues through dialogue are ignored, missed or avoided.

When Natalia was asked to take on a management role in the department, she quickly realized that she would have to speak to Serge about the impact his jokes and stories were having on people in the department.

Natalia inherited a situation that should have been dealt with years ago by previous managers. If you are asked to take over a toxic department or unit, it can be a tough job because you will inherit something you did not create, an environment oozing favouritism, patronage, and inauthentic communication.

But if you work out a strategic plan to systematically address each issue as you engage and communicate with your staff, you will sense a sigh of relief from many who have felt powerless and unheard.

Ed Catmull, the CEO of Pixar and author of *Creativity Inc.*, describes it this way: *so when problems arise—and they always do—disentangling them is not as simple as correcting the original error. Often, finding a solution is a multi-step endeavour. There is the problem you know you are trying to solve—think of that as an oak tree—and then there are all the other problems—think of these as saplings—that sprouted from the acorns that fell around it. And these problems remain after you cut the oak tree down.*

Notes to help you navigate tough conversations

The following section includes notes and observations to help you prepare for tough conversations:

- Compromise, collaboration, cooperation
- What to do when issues appear to be polarized and emotive
- Power imbalances
- Authentic personal power
- Three examples of issues that require tough conversations

Compromise, collaboration, cooperation

When persuading others about tough issues, people generally compromise, collaborate, cooperate, push back strongly or avoid the issue entirely.

As a leader, you need to be mindful of your default patterns when you are faced with tough conversations.

For example, if you have a habit of always trying to find a compromise, you could end up:

- ⬥ giving up something you value such as a work ethic or integrity; or
- ⬥ interpreting policy in a way to favour a person or group to reach a solution (of sorts).

Here are three brief explanations of compromise, collaboration and cooperation:

Compromise

When you compromise, you embrace both assertiveness and cooperation. It's not an ideal approach but you get results when you choose to compromise to solve issues that are of moderate importance to you and the other person or group. And if the other person feels strongly about their position and you don't feel strongly about yours, then it's appropriate to compromise. (Based broadly on the research of Dr. Kenneth W. Thomas and Dr. Ralph H. Kilmann)

Collaboration

The goal is to build an acceptable solution by shifting from entrenched positions towards a collaborative approach. It works best when you and the other person or group feel strongly about an issue and everyone is willing to shift positions to build common ground based on shared interests. Collaborating on every issue that comes up takes time and momentum can be lost. If everyone is in agreement, it makes collaboration impotent: healthy differences make collaboration more effective. (Based broadly on the research of Dr. Kenneth W. Thomas and Dr. Ralph H. Kilmann.)

Cooperation

Cooperation is more than collaboration. It's when everybody works together to achieve a mutually beneficial outcome. You jointly search for creative solutions that can satisfy the needs of each person or group rather than focusing on competing solutions that involve trade-offs or compromise. When people cooperate, it's because everyone has the same idea and their interests, motivations and approach are rooted in common ground.

⇔⇔⇔

What to do when issues appear to be polarized and emotive

Interests can be common, or different or competing. If a conversation becomes polarized or stuck, or if an employee becomes entrenched in a position, integrate the following techniques into your tough conversation:

1. Let the other person vent, acknowledge their views and continue to listen actively
2. Gauge the emotional temperature
3. Focus on an inside-out approach by finding the centre of the conversation
4. Park judgment and be aware of your assumptions
5. Reframe and paraphrase the other person's comments to make sure you hear them
6. Slice a larger issue into smaller pieces
7. Depersonalize the issue by separating it from people
8. Listen without judgment and tease out their interests or concerns
9. Reduce the interests or concerns to three or four key points
10. Check for understanding as you go along
11. Express your own interests and concerns
12. Acknowledge differences
13. Establish common ground based on shared interests
14. Decide on an action plan based on shared interests

When an issue is complex or you have inherited a situation where certain behaviours and attitudes have gone unchecked for years, there will be no easy solution. Don't shy away from emotive outbursts—emotions are a natural part of self-expression.

Allow the person to vent. Pause the conversation if needed for a short while but don't delay dealing with the issues. Usually after an emotional outburst, an opportunity for a productive outcome reveals itself.

Be prepared to have a series of *Necessary Conversations* before you decide to have a *Tough Conversation*.

It might also be appropriate to ask your colleague to request feedback from three or four colleagues using the *From Growth to Great* method and to document the feedback. The feedback will provide you and your colleague with context and examples to help find a solution through *The Tough Conversation* process.

⇔⇔⇔

Notes on power imbalances

It's important for leaders to identify and understand how power plays out at work, especially power imbalances. Nick Morgan, author of *Understand the Four Components of Influence*, says *people with power over others tend to talk more, to interrupt more, and to guide the conversation more*.

Leaders need to get involved when a power imbalance that has negative impacts on others becomes dysfunctional—when participants, either knowingly or unknowingly, give up something of their personhood and authenticity to make the relationship work. These power imbalances can be subtle and covert, or overt and direct.

For every organization to function, a hierarchy of power is necessary. Paramilitary, police, military and emergency services rely on power imbalances—a chain of command to ensure projects and challenges are carried out efficiently and effectively.

My focus is on imbalances of power at work or home that are dysfunctional: when a person shifts to or operates from a *Power-Over* position and the respondent adopts or is forced into a *Power-Less* position to keep the relationship going, keep their job or achieve some type of compromised outcome.

Explanations of power imbalances – Power-Over and Power-Less

A hierarchy of power is necessary for an organization to function. It's when power is abused within the natural, functioning hierarchy of an organization, that we need to pay attention to *Power-Over* and *Power-Less* imbalances.

The person who adopts a *Power-Over* position (e.g. a bully) can hook a person in a *Power-Less* position (e.g. a victim) or the other way around. A person in a *Power-Less* position (e.g. a masochist) can hook a person in a *Power-Over* position (e.g. a rescuer) and build a co-dependent relationship.

When power imbalances are enacted repeatedly with the same participants or group of people, both the *Power-Over* and the *Power-Less* become hooked in a type of co-dependency.

Either the *Power-Over* or the *Power-Less* position can initiate an interaction. These interactions can be over in 30 seconds or play out repeatedly for years if left unchecked.

A *Power-Over* position is an imposition of power that's abused and unnecessary to communicate, collaborate and get things done. A *Power-Over* position is a violation of civil norms that hides an agenda of manipulation, narcissism, neuroticism and reward-seeking.

Sometimes a *Power-Less* position hides an agenda of victimhood, always being aggrieved and avoiding responsibility. A person who is not assertive and always gives up something to accommodate pressure from a boss or colleague is often unaware (no agenda) that they slip into a *Power-Less* position to enable a relationship of sorts to function.

A *Power-Less* person can come across as a victim but could be a *Power-Over* position in disguise. These people operate from an appearance of being one-down or *Power-Less* but specialize in manipulation, passive aggression or *Power-Over* behaviours to get attention or rewards.

These examples might sound strange, but power imbalances exist in most organizations—some more extreme than others. Leaders need to recognize power imbalances at work, especially power imbalances that have become co-dependencies.

This requires interrupting patterns that impact negatively on staff. That means having *Necessary Conversations* with *Power-Over* and *Power-Less* staff and coaching *Power-Less people* on how to find their voice, step into their *Authentic Power* (to be explained later in this chapter) and become assertive at work.

It is important for leaders to coach employees in dysfunctional power imbalances to be aware of the imbalance and its negative impacts and to encourage a growth approach that results in more authentic, clear and engaged relationships.

When you step into your personal power, you interrupt abuses of power and show up as credible, authentic, clear and engaged—your *Authentic Power* mode.

A power imbalances self-check

Think about your work environment. What do you notice about the way you show up? What power imbalances are happening at work that need to be addressed? What changes do you need to make?

Examples of power imbalances

One-off occurrences of power imbalances are nothing to be concerned about. As a leader, you need to be aware of repetitive power imbalances that impact relationships, productivity and morale at work.

1. The Rescuer – a person who adopts a *Power-Over* position person finds meaning and satisfaction helping a *Power-Less* person. The *Power-Over* person needs a *Power-Less* person for a sense of identity but can run out of emotional and psychological energy if the needs of a *Power-Less* person become too demanding or overwhelming.

2. The Manipulator – a manipulator will often come across as a victim and communicate as a *Power-Less* person. In reality, a manipulator is a *Power-Over* person because their goal is to manipulate anyone they come across. Manipulators are successful when a relationship builds between them and

a willing supporter who genuinely wants to help and unwittingly adopts a *Power-Over* position in relation to the manipulator, who comes across as *Power-Less*. The willing supporter is often unaware of what's really going on and provides material support or gives something up of themselves to make the relationship work.

3. The Expert – an expert in this sense uses their experience to advantage. They come across as having a unique perspective and knowledge on a wide range of topics—a *Power-Over* position—and are dismissive of those—the *Power-Less*—who don't have the same years of experience or who haven't worked their way up through the system as they have. An expert who comes across as a *Power-Over* person will often use up all the airtime to wax eloquent on a range of topics. A *Power-Over* expert loves the attention of willing *Power-Less* people who fail to see through the haze of bafflegab and assess the relationship for what it really is.

4. The Bully – the bully, operating out of a *Power-Over* mode, intimidates a person who adopts a *Power-Less* position. Leaders need to act swiftly and interrupt all bullying behaviours. This involves having *Necessary* and or *Tough Conversations* with the bully and engaging in compassionate, empathic and helpful conversations with the *Power-Less* person who is being bullied. It includes having *Necessary Conversations* with the victim and helping them step into their *Authentic Power* (to be explained in a moment), find their voice and become assertive at work.

Less obvious forms of bullying at work are withholding or providing incorrect information, hiding the success of the person being bullied, using performance reviews as leverage, undermining work and many others. Bullying is a sustained form of psychological or sometimes physical abuse that aims to make the victim feel demeaned and inadequate. It's experienced as offensive, malicious or insulting behaviour. Bullying intimidates, belittles and humiliating the recipient, leading to loss of self-esteem for the victim.

5. The Victim – the victim in this power imbalance is not a genuine victim of abuse, bullying, disenfranchisement or harassment but a person who assumes the role of victim to pursue or manipulate an agenda. The victim needs to continually adopt a position of powerlessness to attract attention and build momentum for their cause. For the *Power-Less* imbalance to work, the victim needs a group, organization or an individual to align with or identify with their story. A person who comes to a victim's aid often has a big heart and a genuine desire to make the world a better place. When this person gets hooked into the victim's story, they unconsciously shift into a rescue mode—a soft *Power-Over* position.

The good-hearted *Power-Over* person can often end up giving their time, money, resources—and in extreme cases—sacrificing their values and self-respect to help out.

If left unchecked, a person playing a victim role at work can manipulate unsuspecting people. Over time this behaviour de-energizes the office environment and damages team morale and relationships.

6. The Passive Aggressive - passive aggressive behaviour can vary in severity, frequency and intentionality. If not addressed, it will slowly erode team spirit and divide an inclusive and authentic work culture.

A passive aggressive person uses power imbalances similar to the *Manipulator* or *Victim*: they come across as *Power-Less* but in effect operate from a disguised position of *Power-Over* others.

For example, when a person who uses passive aggression is given a task to do that they don't agree with, they will come across as supportive and agreeable without disclosing that they have reservations about doing it or are feeling disappointed or angry about the task.

Instead of speaking openly and honestly about how they feel in the moment, they will select a few unsuspecting colleagues and let them know how unfairly they've been treated. They come across as a *Power-Less* victim who has been unfairly treated. This victim persona will then try to manipulate the situation to their advantage—seeking compensation as payback with special concessions such as time off, shorter hours or reduced workload.

This passive aggressive behaviour sends mixed messages to everyone involved in a project, because the person shows up as a *Power-Less* victim but in reality, manipulates an agenda for self-benefit and *Power-Over* others. This makes everyone feel uneasy because they don't know how to address the disconnect between the various personas—the nice person on the surface and the underlying victim and manipulator who operates below the radar of authenticity.

Various forms of passive aggressive *Power-Over* manipulation and payback include:
- Intentional ineffectiveness
- Intentional lateness and forgetfulness
- Sulkiness

- Sabotage of projects and deadlines
- Undermining colleagues behind their back
- Indirect criticism
- Mixed messages that hint of a conspiracy against them
- Providing incorrect information
- Withholding information
- Moving goal posts

An employee who uses passive aggression will send mixed messages and come across as:

- Feeling under-appreciated.
- Lacking accountability, placing blame on others.
- Procrastinating or missing deadlines.
- Grumpy or irritable but won't say why.
- Using indirect means of communication in difficult situations.

Counselling Directory – UK – adapted

⇔⇔⇔

Authentic personal power

The antidote to power imbalances is to communicate assertively using your authentic personal power—*Authentic Power*. The six power imbalances illustrating *Power-Over* and *Power-Less* scenarios are examples of dysfunctional power at work or home. Using your authentic personal power can counteract power imbalances, especially when the passion you display for the truth is based on evidence and your communication is calm, measured and professional.

So, don't underestimate the power of your personality and the way you come across when you have a tough conversation. Finding your voice and having healthy self-esteem has a big impact on your personal power—

your ability to persuade others to find common ground in tough conversations and agree on a solution.

Assertiveness means expressing your point of view clearly and directly, while still respecting others. When you find your voice and stand in your *Authentic Power*, you can engage in tough conversations, hear the concerns of others and advocate for a fair solution in a professional way without bruising relationships.

Being assertive and communicating with your authentic personal power includes:
- persuading others with genuine emotion and passion (emotional power);
- being well prepared and organised (professional power); and
- being articulate and clear about the purpose of a tough conversation, while acknowledging differences and building on common interests or whys (conversational power).

⇔⇔⇔

Preparing for your Tough Conversation

Here are seven guidelines to help you prepare for your Tough Conversation:

1. The *Reason* for the conversation and expected *Result*

Clarify and communicate in advance the *Reason* for the conversation and the expected *Result*.

Once you are clear about the *Reason* and *Result*, don't delay sending the email and setting up a time for the conversation. Resist the temptation to smooth things over or get through it as possible, because of your discomfort with tough conversations.

2. Perspectives

Anticipate the other person's perspective and clarify your point of view. Don't waste time thinking through what you are going to say. Use the four anchors and key words of the LEAD conversation as a guide but don't memorize statements or phrases. Adopt a quiet confidence in the LEAD process. View the Tough Conversation as a personal growth opportunity and anticipate a productive outcome rather than a negative experience to be endured.

3. Model the behaviours

Model the behaviours of a leader and come out, as it were, for all staff so everyone feels accepted, no matter their background, culture, religion, gender and physical ability.

4. Mindset of curiosity

Stay curious throughout the conversation and be mindful of not labeling any behaviour as a judgment. Be aware of the story you make up about the other person. Remain open-minded and be curious, especially when new information contradicts your perspective, belief or mindset. Be curious about your role (if any) that could have caused or aggravated the situation. Be prepared to probe beyond symptoms for driving interests.

5. Respectful truthfulness

It's important to respectfully hear what the other person is saying (and not saying) while not tiptoeing around the issue that needs to be resolved. Be truthful about addressing the issues without bruising the relationship. If you show respect and communicate truthfully, the chances are you will generate a similar response from the other person.

6. Empathy and self-empathy—Emotion and Meaning

Empathize with the other person (empathy is not agreement) and try to see things from their perspective: imagine the *Emotion* they are going through and what the outcome could *Mean* to them. It could mean that the other person has to make real, measurable changes to their behaviour as there will be consequences for inaction.

Self-empathy—what are you feeling—the *Emotion*—and what does this conversation *Mean* to you? Could it blow up into something bigger? Does it mean it can be resolved if dealt with appropriately? It could mean you are taking appropriate steps and this will build your confidence, however uncomfortable it is to have a tough conversation.

7. Anticipate the future

If you don't address these behaviours, what are the anticipated costs to your team such as morale, productivity and potential loss of key staff? Is this conflict? Can it lead to more conflict with staff if it's not addressed? Aim for a growth-oriented and positive outcome.

⇔⇔⇔

Three examples of issues that require tough conversations

The following three examples require *Tough Conversations* to resolve the issues.

Before you have the *Tough Conversation*, think about how you would communicate the *Reason* for the conversation and the expected *Result* at the end of each conversation.

1. The disrespectful colleague

Serge has an energizing, extroverted personality. He is liked by staff and comes across as the joker of the group. It bothers you that Serge, while popular, shows 'respect' to certain groups but behind the scenes, mocks and insults them. These jokes are often about religion, members of the LGBTQ community and are often tinged with subtle racism.

You have already had a Necessary Conversation with Serge but there has been no change in behaviour.

You need to have a Tough Conversation with Serge

- ❖ The Reason—*Serge, I'd like to follow up on our previous conversation and talk about how you come across to your colleagues.*
- ❖ Result—*My hope is that you will see this as a growth opportunity and commit to different ways of communicating going forward.*

2. The colleague who has a drinking problem

Wanda is a recovering alcoholic. She has made it public and has the support of everyone on the team. Recently staff have reported to you that Wanda has been showing up at work smelling of alcohol.

You immediately addressed this with Wanda and things went back to normal. But now it's becoming a weekly occurrence—with reports of Wanda coming back from lunch in an inebriated state.

You have already had several *Necessary Conversations* with Wanda to address this issue. Nothing has changed. Now, you need to prepare for and have a *Tough Conversation* with Wanda.

You need to have a *Tough Conversation* with Wanda
- ✧ The Reason—*As you know Wanda, we've had several conversations about the impact that drinking alcohol, especially during work hours, is having on your work and colleagues. I'd like to meet with you tomorrow, if possible.*
- ✧ Result—*I want this to be resolved permanently so that there's no need for further action that could impact on your career.*

3. The employee who manipulates the system

You recently took over as manager of a department within your organization. You noticed that Devin refuses to do any work that falls, even slightly, outside of his job description.

Devin resists all efforts to upgrade his job description and constantly threatens legal action with the support of his employee union.

It seems as if Devin knows how to manipulate the system—drawing attention to his rights without acting on any responsibilities as an employee.

Your department is undergoing change. There is constant pressure to deliver results to your stakeholders. There are many projects with different timelines. Everyone on the team, except Devin, works extra hours when a job needs to be done. These assignments need dedicated leaders who are willing and able to manage projects every step of the way.

You have already had several *Necessary Conversations* with Devin to address this issue. Nothing has changed. Now you need to prepare for and have a *Tough Conversation* with Devin.

You need to have a *Tough Conversation* with Devin

- ✧ The Reason—*Devin, I'd like to get together with you and talk about your rights and your areas of responsibility. We need to clarify what you are responsible for and what my expectations are on how you deliver on them.*
- ✧ Result—*I would like to end up where both of us agree on what you are accountable for and find an action-oriented solution that both of us can live with—something that's fair and actionable.*

Dene Rossouw

The Mentoring Conversation

The Mentoring Conversation
List of topics in this chapter

- ✧ When to use *The Mentoring Conversation*
- ✧ A mentoring approach
- ✧ Learning styles
- ✧ The Mentoring Conversation
- ✧ The Mentoring Conversation example—Kat and Angeline
- ✧ Mentoring conversation topics

*T*he *Mentoring Conversation* is a hybrid approach that combines elements of mentoring and coaching into a conversation that invites growth and possibility. Successful mentoring is an art.

The Mentoring Conversation consists of five steps. Using the mnemonic GREAT—the Mentoring Conversation provides structure to help you have meaningful conversations on just about any mentoring topic. The five steps are:

- ⟡ Goals—Clarify your mentoring topic and objectives
- ⟡ Reality—Explore challenges your learning partner is facing
- ⟡ Explore—Search for practical tips and techniques and how to implement
- ⟡ Act—Set specific action steps
- ⟡ Track—Track progress and set key milestones

When to use *The Mentoring Conversation*

The Mentoring Conversation helps you mentor for results and performance using an approach that combines elements of mentoring and coaching into conversations that invite growth and possibility. Each time you meet with your learning partner, direct report or colleague, *The Mentoring Conversation* provides a structured approach to help them reach goals, gain skills mastery and build competencies. It will help you help them be inspired, energised and achieve measurable and meaningful outcomes.

A mentoring approach

Mentoring is about co-learning in a collaborative environment and involves creating a learning partnership. Both you (the mentor) and your colleague (your learning partner) discover answers together.

Being a mentor means you value learning. You ask insightful questions that challenge your learning partner to expand their horizons of possibility. Essential ingredients are excellent listening skills and the willingness to share your knowledge, skills, experiences and perspectives to foster the personal and professional growth of your learning partner.

The Mentoring Conversation involves reframing challenges and issues, introducing new ways of doing things and suggesting new approaches to old paradigms. You help identify non-productive patterns and behaviours and draw on storytelling to illustrate learning points from your experience of the workplace.

Your role as a mentor is best described as a balance between being a learning advisor (instructive) and a motivational coach (curious).

Being instructive includes storytelling, teaching about products, processes, people and personal experiences. Being curious involves deep listening and inquiry about products, processes, people and personal experiences. Being instructive and curious help to lead your learning partner to insight and action.

You need to be a role model: coaching is first caught, then taught. It is important that you see self-disclosure about your successes, challenges and failures as integral to your role as a mentor.

This is not a call to perfection but as a mentor of others, you must be authentic, walk the talk and be an example.

Your role as a mentor is to:
1. Model the competencies of leadership and be open to discuss uncomfortable realities when necessary.
2. Help your learning partner identify the skills needed to become competent—to be a persuasive presenter at conferences, for example.
3. Help your learning partner gain mastery of skills with a mentoring process that's relevant and engaging.
4. Create a safe space and dedicated time for dialogue. A mentoring conversation should promote learning where your learning partner feels heard and their opinions matter.
5. Suggest changes to personal goals and key result areas as the environment changes.

A mentoring conversation can be about any subject, such as goals, leadership style, working with difficult employees, time management and so on. It's important for your learning partner to take ownership of the opportunity and to commit to a successful outcome.

⇔⇔⇔

Learning styles

Before we get into the structure of a mentoring conversation, you need to be aware of your own and your partner's learning styles.

Learning styles are different ways of taking in and understanding information. These styles are affected by a range of factors including age, experience, physiology and culture.

How people learn can be better remembered and understood as five integrated ways of building skills and competencies. I use the mnemonic AWARE to help you remember the five learning styles.

Be AWARE of your own preferred styles and try and discover and capitalize on the preferred learning styles of your learning partner—Act, Watch, Attention, Read & Record and Experiment:

- Act—help your learning partner learn by giving them an assignment to solve a problem or challenge
- Watch—help your learning partner learn by asking them to watch instructive videos and report back to you on key aspects aligned with their mentoring goals
- Attention—help your learning partner learn by giving them an assignment to pay focused attention on any subject matter and report back to you on key insights
- Read and record—help your learning partner learn by giving them an assignment to write or type up subject matter aligned with their mentoring goals
- Experiment—help your learning partner learn by giving them an assignment to innovate, discover and explore possibilities

There's no one size that fits all learners. It's important to be conscious of your own learning style as a leader and be prepared to adapt or let go of your style to accommodate the learning styles of your colleagues and learning partners.

The Mentoring Conversation

The Mentoring Conversation consists of five steps using the mnemonic *GREAT*:

- Goals—Clarify your mentoring topic and objectives
- Reality—Explore challenges your learning partner is facing
- Explore—Search for practical tips and techniques and how to implement
- Act—Set specific action steps
- Track—Track progress and set key milestones

The five steps or anchors that guide your mentoring conversation provide structure for your conversations on just about any mentoring topic so you don't go off track and dilute the process and impact.

The five-step path is designed to help your learning partner achieve measurable and realistic outcomes. The conversational anchors (GREAT) serve as a guide as you ask insightful questions that challenge your learning partner to expand their horizons of possibility. It's about integrating two essential mentoring practices: being instructive and remaining curious.

The mentoring topic can be anything your learning partner wants to work on: time management, career advancement, leading effective meetings, giving presentations etc.

The Mentoring Conversation should always start with a brief check-in. Talk briefly about what's going on with you as well. Then go through each of the GREAT steps and conclude with a brief wrap-up at the end of the session.

Suggested questions are listed within each of the GREAT mentoring steps. For clarity, we have included just two questions for each anchor point. Add your own insightful questions and secondary questions as the mentoring conversation progresses. Only ask those questions that are relevant to your learning partner.

Check-in

Greet and confirm time available. Have a brief check-in on what's going on.

Goals—Clarify the goals of your mentoring topic

What are your goals?

(The first time you meet, talk about career and life goals. Thereafter, goals should be topic specific such as *Managing and leading people* or *Leading effective meetings* and so on.)

What will be different when you reach your goals?

Reality—Explore challenges your learning partner is facing

What challenges are you facing?

What is the downside if you don't make these changes?

Explore—Search for practical tips and techniques and how to implement

What ideas do you have?

How can you put them into practice?

Act—Set specific action steps

What do you think you should do next?

When will you start?

Track—Track progress and set key milestones

How will we track progress?

What are key progress milestones?

Wrap up

Give and invite feedback on how the mentoring session went. Set up a time and date for the next session.

⇔ ⇔ ⇔

The Mentoring Conversation example—Kat and Angeline

Kat is a director of an asset management company that specializes in investments in green technologies. Angeline is a portfolio manager and has been with the company for two years.

Kat has been mentoring Angeline—a rising star—for nine months on specialist skills and topics required for being a successful portfolio manager.

Kat is about to have a mentoring conversation with Angeline on how to present with more impact to her existing and potential clients who want to invest in the green energy sector.

Brief check-in

Hi, Angeline. It's good to see you again. How's your week going so far? (Brief check-in)

"Hi, Kat, it's been awhile. This week I've started a new project and I'm so excited about that. I so look forward to these mentoring sessions."

Same here, Angeline. I'm glad I was able to book the boardroom for our session. It's a familiar environment for you, as so many of our client presentations happen here.

Goals—Clarify the goals of your mentoring topic

So, you mentioned you would like to improve your presentations to clients. Tell me more.

"That's right, Kat. I've watched you a lot and I realize I need to come across more confident and have more of an impact when I present to our clients."

We can work on that for sure, Angeline. What will be different when we are done? Or how will you come across to clients when you feel you have reached your goal?

"I'll come across more persuasively and with more clarity. And I'll tell stories that are more strategic and compelling that lead to a call to action."

Okay, I'm writing these all down. I'm glad you mentioned storytelling because researching and sharing insightful stories that help our clients make better decisions is one of the key things we do effectively here.

Reality—Explore challenges your learning partner is facing
I've sat in on quite a few of your presentations, Angeline. But take me through your reality. What challenges are you facing that you want to overcome?

"First of all, I take way too long to prepare a presentation for a new client. I muddle around and get so stressed out. If I think about it, I don't know where to start."

Feeling anxious about a presentation has a direct link to your level of confidence. What else is a challenge for you?

"I second-guess myself and that results in offering the client too many options. I guess I want to please them and show I've done my homework. But the result is they tend to delay making an investment decision because they now want to think about all the options I've provided."

I've also done that in the past, Angeline. I can certainly help you with that. What's the downside if you don't make these changes to your presentations?

"My learning curve will take forever. I'll not have as much success with new business and reach the assets under management goal we set three months ago. And that impacts not only me but the whole team."

Explore—Search for practical tips and techniques and how to implement

Okay, so to summarize so far, you want to have a more powerful impact when you present to clients, you would like to feel more confident, you'd like to have a strategy to prepare your presentations, you want to offer fewer but more compelling options that lead to more investment decisions and finally, you want to tell stories that lead to a call to action? Is that it?

"It sounds so much, Angeline. This might take years."

They are all linked in some way, Kat. I'd like to start off with the foundation of all compelling presentations, and that's the preparation. And it won't take years, you'll see.

"I'm all ears."

I'll send you a template I use. It will be a suggested outline and checklist but only for the conclusion of your presentation.

"Just the conclusion?"

I know it sounds strange and counterintuitive, but when you prepare a presentation, you need to prepare the conclusion first. No introduction, no body. Nothing else but the conclusion.
Can you think what might be the advantage of doing it this way?

"I guess it forces you to focus on what you want the client to know, the benefits, the value you bring and the call to action."

Precisely. You've got it.

Act—Set specific action steps

So, I'm going to send you this outline to help you build out the conclusion of your next presentation. It's my understanding you have a new client presentation in three weeks?

"That's right."

Great. So, what do you think you should do next—your first priority?

"I'm going to use the template you send me and build out the conclusion of my presentation."

Now don't worry about all the other things we spoke about like stories and so on. We'll deal with those once you've built out the conclusion.

Track—Track progress and set key milestones

I'd like you to come in early next week and present just the conclusion to me. I'll be an audience of one. Can you be ready to go at 7:30 am this coming Tuesday?

"I'll be here, Kat. Wow, I'm feeling a bit nervous now but this is good. I'm looking forward to it."

No need to feel nervous at all, Angeline. I'll provide you with feedback, focusing on growth areas first and then I'll shift to things you are doing well. Please set aside Tuesday and Friday mornings at 7:30am for the next few weeks. We'll build in the other elements you want to improve on so that you'll be ready and much more confident when your client presentations come around.

"Thanks for your time, Kat. I so appreciate you sharing your expertise with me."

⇔⇔⇔

Mentoring conversation topics

The five conversational anchors—GREAT—can be used to guide just about any mentoring topic.

Here are 14 potential mentoring conversation topics:
1. Career goals and challenges.
2. Best practice self-management.
3. Managing and leading people.
4. Better collaboration and teamwork.
5. Dealing with difficult personalities.
6. Best practice project management.
7. Improving customer service.
8. Effective communication skills.
9. Presenting with more impact.
10. Giving and asking for feedback.
11. How to be more innovative at work.
12. Leading effective meetings.
13. Better time management.
14. How to perform tasks specific to a department or tasks that follow a unique set of guidelines, rules or processes.

⇔⇔⇔

Conclusion

The advice, tools and templates in *Credible* are intended to help you feel more confident expressing yourself and influencing others. As you use the tools provided for each conversation, with practice, they will become intuitive and second nature to you.

I hope that you never shrink back, but instead, seize the opportunity to have impactful leadership conversations when the moment presents itself.

Take delight in your ability to make a big difference, one conversation at a time.

The Six Leadership Conversations:

1. The Listening Conversation—helps you have a meaningful conversation with anyone who feels strongly about an issue, or wants to change or initiate something

2. The Learning Conversation—helps you coach anyone who seeks a solution to a challenge, problem or issue, by helping them take ownership of it, come to insight and take action

3. The Feedback Conversation—helps you ask for feedback from a colleague, or provide feedback to a colleague, using an approach that's specific, positive and growth-oriented

4. The Necessary Conversation—helps you have a meaningful dialogue with someone to address a challenge, resolve an issue or problem or a misunderstanding and agree on an action

5. The Tough Conversation—helps you have a structured conversation and document a course of action to resolve misunderstandings, deal with conflict and entrenched behaviours that cause disruption and deplete morale at work

6. The Mentoring Conversation—helps you mentor for results and performance using an approach that combines elements of mentoring and coaching into conversations that invite growth and possibility

About the Author

Dene Rossouw is the
Principal Learning Facilitator at Team Possibil.com.
He has facilitated hundreds of programs for various organizations in
Africa and Canada and is known for his ability to demystify complexity
and explain processes using transferable concepts and dynamic models.
He lives on Vancouver Island and is an avid wildlife photographer.

The Six Leadership Conversations

www.ingramcontent.com/pod-product-compliance
Lightning Source LLC
Chambersburg PA
CBHW060835220526
45466CB00003B/1108